Step-by-Step Cooking

Soups & Sauces

Marshall Cavendish London & New York

Pictures supplied by

Rex Bamber	53, 56, 57, 58, 59, 60/1, 65, 66, 67
Alan Duns	21, 22/3, 28/9, 31, 32, 33, 36, 37, 38, 39, 40, 70, 71, 89, 90, 91, 96
Melvin Grey	8, 9, 20, 78
Paul Kemp	1, 11, 14, 41, 47, 48, 49, 50, 51
David Levin	3, 4, 5, 6, 10, 12/3, 15, 30, 34, 35, 43, 46, 47(t), 54, 55, 62, 63, 64, 68, 69, 72, 75, 76, 77, 79, 82, 83, 92, 94, 95
Peter Lloyd	85, 86, 87, 88
Roger Phillips	52, 80, 81
George Wright	17, 18, 19, 44

Published by
Marshall Cavendish Books Limited
58 Old Compton Street
London W1V 5PA

© Marshall Cavendish Limited 1977, 1978

This material was first published by
Marshall Cavendish Limited
in the partwork *Good Cooking*.

Printed in Great Britain by Alabaster Passmore & Sons Ltd

ISBN 0 85685 440 9

Introduction

The art of making good soups and sauces is essential to know and easy to acquire. Soup can be prepared from everyday ingredients in less than an hour and served with crusty bread to provide a satisfying meal for unexpected guests. A sauce can be made even more quickly and can turn leftovers into a luxury dish or give convenience food an individual touch that shows you care.

Both soups and sauces are frequently based on stock, so that is where *Step-by-Step Cooking Soups and Sauces* begins. Stocks are simple and cheap to prepare and easy to store, and are used in so many different dishes, from soups and sauces to casseroles and stews, that their special flavours can turn simple dishes into something special. Every cook should keep a reserve supply.

Soups, savoury or sweet, substantial or delicate, cold or hot, are so versatile that they can be used as elegant starters to a formal meal or as meals in themselves. This tempting array of recipes ranges from the improvised and economic to the sophisticated and classic. Whatever the occasion or the time of year soup is always an appropriate part of a meal.

Sauces are equally flexible and may be sweet or savoury, thick or thin, white or coloured. Whether you are serving cauliflower, fillet steak or ice-cream, a good sauce will add to both the appearance and flavour of the dish and give a professional touch to your cooking.

Soups and sauces are two of the 'basics' of good cooking which also make for good eating.

Time symbols: an indication of preparation and cooking time is given for each recipe. This is calculated for beginners new to the techniques involved; experienced cooks can allow less time.

        ☒   less than 1 hour
      ☒☒ 1-2½ hours
    ☒☒☒ over 2½ hours

Weights and measures: both metric and Imperial measurements are given throughout, with Imperial figures appearing in square brackets. Metric and Imperial measures are not exact equivalents so be sure to work with only one or other set of figures.

Soups and Sauces

Contents

Home-made stock bases 1

Hearty soups 11

Purée soups 22

Cream soups 31

White roux-based and sweet sauces 41

Velouté sauces 53

Brown sauces 65

Mayonnaise and emulsion sauces 79

Egg and butter sauces 89

Index 97

Soups

home-made stock bases

Home-made stock is one of the 'basics' of good cookery. It is easy and satisfying to make and it can do a great deal to enhance simple everyday cooking, and to give soups and sauces authentic flavour.

WHAT IS STOCK?

Basically, stock is a liquid obtained by simmering meat or fish bones and trimmings in water with herbs, vegetables and seasonings. When all the goodness and flavour have been extracted, the liquid is strained and reduced to concentrate flavour. The resulting stock is then used as a base for soups, sauces, casseroles, aspics, stews and gravies.

Why make stock yourself when you can buy stock cubes? The answer is flavour. Without good stocks, many of the world's greatest dishes would not be worth tasting.

Making your own stock is, of course, more time-consuming than simply dissolving a stock cube in boiling water but the extra effort involved is not very great, and there is a world of difference in taste and texture. Stock cubes contain large amounts of salt and monosodium glutamate (an artificial flavouring) to give them a longer shelf life. These strong flavours concentrate during cooking and can easily spoil a delicate sauce or soup.

Types of stock

Stocks are divided into two types – brown and white. Brown stocks are richly coloured because the ingredients are lightly fried before liquid is added, while white stocks are more delicate in colour and in flavour.

Stocks are also divided into categories according to the quality of ingredients used. First stocks are the finest, made from fresh ingredients and usually used for sauces, soups and aspics where a really top-quality stock is essential. Second stocks are made from bones which have already been used once in stockmaking (with the addition of a few fresh ingredients to bolster flavour). Not so fine in flavour as first stocks, they are perfectly suitable for stews and casseroles and simple sauces.

Like most thin soups, spicy hot and sour soup is cooked very quickly so a good, well-flavoured brown stock is needed.

Types of stock & their uses

Stock	Uses
Brown stock: so called because ingredients are coloured by browning in fat before water is added. It is usually made exclusively from beef bones and meat, plus celery, onions or leeks, carrots and herbs. You may however, find some recipes which include veal or chicken.	The ideal choice for brown sauces. Also for kidney, tomato and vegetable soups requiring good colour and strong flavour, for moistening red meat casseroles and pies and, if very meaty and well-flavoured, for aspics, clear hot and cold jellied soups.
Game stock: a brown stock made from game carcasses and meat scraps plus beef bones (fresh or saved from making brown stock) plus vegetables, particularly celery, and complementary herbs.	Distinctive game flavour. Use for game soups, sauces to serve with game and to moisten game pies, pâtés and casseroles.
White stock: usually made from the bones and meat scraps of one or several of the following: veal, chicken, rabbit, pork, mutton, lamb, and ham, plus celery, root vegetables and herbs. Omit mutton, lamb and ham for a general-purpose white stock and only use pork sparingly.	Delicate meaty flavour and pale colour if based on veal or chicken. Use for cream soups, fine white sauces and aspics. A stock containing a lot of lamb or mutton is ideal for Scotch and barley broths. Use ham stocks for soups and purées made with peas or other pulses.
Household stock: white stock made from bones of a cooked ham, lamb or veal joint or chicken carcass plus any raw or cooked trimmings. Giblets, bacon rinds and scraps plus vegetables and herbs are also added.	Pale in colour. Not as fine in flavour as white stock but very economical and useful for vegetable broths, simple white sauces and casseroles made with pork or veal.
Chicken stock: white stock made with boiling fowl and knuckle of veal for maximum flavour. Cheaper versions use carcass, skin and giblets plus poultry scraps; or giblets only. Always include celery, a few root vegetables and herbs.	Good poultry flavour, pale colour. An excellent general-purpose stock for all types of soups, sauces for vegetables and white meat dishes, moistening white meat casseroles and pies and boiling rice for savoury dishes or for risottos.
Fish stock: a white stock made with heads, bones and trimmings of white fish, lemon, celery, a few root vegetables and herbs. Turbot heads, halibut, sole and plaice bones are best. Add cheap fresh white fish to bolster flavour if bones are few.	Almost colourless. Delicately flavoured. Quickly made. Wine can replace some of the water. Use immediately for fish soups, poaching fish, fish aspics and sauces or rice to accompany fish dishes.
Vegetable stock: really neither white nor brown. A good way to use up scraps. Can be made from one or several of the following: celery stalks, trimmings from leeks and carrots, outer cabbage leaves, watercress stalks, mushroom peelings, outer lettuce leaves, young pea or broad bean pods and some vegetable cooking liquids.	Mostly used in vegetarian cookery. Colour and flavour can be strengthened by lightly browning vegetables in butter before water is added. Blend all ingredients in a liquidizer to make an instant soup. Or strain off vegetables and use liquid for soups, braising vegetables, cooking pulses and for boiling rice.

CHOOSING INGREDIENTS

The very best first stocks are made from fresh meaty bones (or fish and fish bones) and vegetables bought specifically for the purpose. But there is no need to buy special ingredients for an economic stock for everyday use. Household stock is made by using leftovers which might otherwise go to waste – a cooked joint bone or chicken carcass and vegetable peelings (wrapped and refrigerated these scraps will keep for up to five days).

Do not, however, be tempted to treat your stockpot like a dustbin – throwing all your scraps into it indiscriminately will only produce poor results.

When choosing ingredients for stock, bear in mind the final dishes you plan to use it in. If, for instance, you are planning a chicken casserole, there is no point in including beef bones or cabbage – these distinctive flavours will not harmonize with or complement a chicken dish.

Meat and bones

There is great scope here for obtaining ingredients very cheaply, or even free. When you visit your butcher look out for large bones and odd pieces of meat (often left lying on the slab behind the counter). Most butchers are only too glad to sell them very cheaply and may even give them to you free of charge. Remember when buying bones that they have to fit into a pan so ask for them to be cut up. And, if you buy meat and ask the butcher to bone and trim it for you remember to take bones and trimmings home with you – useful additions for the stockpot.

What kind of meat and bones can you use? All sorts of bones can be used. Those with meat attached give extra flavour and make your stock more nutritious.

Beef bones and trimmings are excellent. Ham, gammon, mutton and lamb bones have distinctive flavour but they are useful for some specific purposes (see Types of Stock and their Uses). Pork bones and meat should be used sparingly as they give stock a slightly sweet flavour. Veal bones, pigs' trotters and calves' heads are excellent if you want a really gelatinous stock, so always include one of these if you want to make aspics or jellied soup. Chicken carcasses and game birds are also good for flavour, particularly if scraps of meat are attached. Bones must always be washed before use and veal must be blanched (plunged into boiling water) for five minutes and then rinsed before use because it releases a mass of grey scum which makes the stock cloudy.

Fish
The bones, heads and trimmings of all raw white fish can be used to make stock. Do not use oily fish (eg mackerel, herring) it is too strong in flavour. Bones and scraps from cooked fish are unsuitable as they have very little flavour to give.

Vegetables
The most commonly used vegetables are onions or leeks, carrots and celery. Always use fresh vegetables or vegetable peelings, never leftover cooked vegetables as these will make stock cloudy. Potatoes and other starchy vegetables, such as peas and beans, may also make stock cloudy and are best avoided.

Mushroom peelings add colour as well as flavour, as do tomatoes, but the latter may sour the stock if kept for more than a day, so it is better to add them only to the final dish. Turnips and members of the cabbage family can be used for vegetable stock but their flavours are too pronounced for meat or fish stock.

Herbs and seasonings
Aromatic and full of flavour, herbs are an essential ingredient of good home-made stock. Salt and peppercorns are also used and, occasionally, mace. Herbs are usually added to stock in the form of a bouquet garni – a little collection of complementary herbs tied together in a bunch if fresh, in a little muslin bag if dried or powdered.

The classic bouquet garni which is suitable for use in all stocks is made up of a sprig of fresh or dried thyme, a dried bay leaf and a few sprigs of fresh parsley. If using powdered herbs, use 5 ml (1 teaspoon) of each. Use a whole dried bay leaf and try to avoid using dried parsley – it is musty and poor in flavour compared to fresh.

You can vary the herbs in a bouquet garni to suit the ingredients in the stock. Do not be tempted to use too many different herbs – their flavours simply cancel each other out and mask rather than enhance the main ingredients.

Rosemary added to a classic bouquet garni is excellent for stocks containing mutton or lamb.
Tarragon either alone or with the classic bouquet garni is good in chicken stock.
Marjoram adds a distinctive flavour to game stocks. A few juniper berries can also be added.
Lemon balm or lemon verbena add pungency to mild chicken or fish stocks.
Fennel is also good for bolstering mild fish stock. Use alone or add it to the classic bouquet garni.

TIMING
Contrary to popular opinion, stock is extremely easy to make. Initial preparation of ingredients and skimming will take you about half an hour. After this, the stock can be left to simmer gently with little or no attention from the cook. Although cooking time can be long (up to five hours for some stocks), it can be stopped and restarted when it suits you. Straining, de-greasing and final flavouring of the stock will take about another 45 minutes or so in all, but once again these jobs can be broken up and done when most convenient. The end product is well worth the effort.

EQUIPMENT
To make stock you will need the following equipment:
● large pan
● skimmer or perforated spoon
● colander
● absorbent kitchen paper
● piece of butter muslin

Making a bouquet garni

1 Collect together a sprig of fresh thyme, a few sprigs of fresh parsley and a bay leaf.

2 Tie into a bunch with cotton, leaving a long end which can be tied to the pan handle.

OR if using dried herbs, place with fresh parsley on a small square of muslin or cheesecloth.

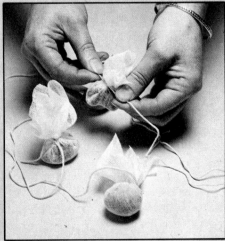

AND gather the edges of the muslin together and tie firmly with cotton, leaving a long end.

Large pan: the pan can be either a conventional saucepan or a double-handled stockpot. It must be heavy-based, lidded and at least 4.6 L [8 pt] capacity. A large size is essential: during cooking, stock reduces by about half, so you have to start with a lot of liquid in order to obtain a reasonable amount of stock.

Skimmer or perforated spoon: this is used to remove scum and sometimes fat from the surface of the stock. A draining spoon used for lifting vegetables out of water can be used but a flat skimmer especially designed for stock is best. You can simply slide the skimmer across the surface of the stock, rather than dipping in, which is necessary with a spoon shape.

Colander: this is used to strain the stock after cooking. As bones and meat tend to be heavy and very hot, a metal colander is best as it will not buckle or warp under the strain and heat.

Kitchen paper: this is used to mop up the fat from the surface of the stock. Double thickness paper is best as it is more absorbent. A slice of white bread can be used instead.

Butter muslin: essential for the final straining of the stock as its fine mesh will trap any scum or particles of food which may have slipped through the colander.

BASIC METHODS

With the exception of brown stock, where initial preparation differs slightly, all stocks are made following the method shown in the step-by-steps on this page. To make brown stock, follow the initial preparation stages shown in the step-by-step on page 6, then continue as for other stocks. Here are a few important points which are relevant to the making of all types of stock.

Bringing to the boil
Bringing the stock to the boil slowly is essential to force out impurities which rise as scum. If you bring the stock to the boil too fast the scum will be driven back into the liquid and will spoil the stock.

Skimming
Once the scum of impurities has formed it must be removed, otherwise it will be re-absorbed by the stock. Lift off the scum using a skimmer or a perforated spoon.

Seasoning
Herbs and seasonings are always added after this initial skimming. Do not season heavily at this stage as the liquid will reduce during cooking and concentrate flavour.

Simmering
Reduce heat to low and half cover the pan with a lid. It is important that the stock simmers (cooks just below boiling point) during the remaining cooking time or fat and scum will amalgamate with the stock and make it cloudy. Let it simmer very gently – just a bubble or two breaking the surface – until the liquid is reduced by almost half. This may take up to five hours (although fish stock should never be cooked for longer than 30 minutes). Skim as necessary during cooking and top up with boiling water if the liquid looks as if it will fall below the level of the ingredients.

Straining and de-greasing
Strain the stock through a colander into a large bowl or another pan, pressing the juices through with a spoon or vegetable press. Discard vegetables and herbs. Keep meat (if used) for potting or making into a cottage pie or Bolognese sauce. Keep bones for making second stock.

If the stock is for immediate use, remove the grease by floating a piece of absorbent kitchen paper or a slice of white bread on the surface. This will absorb the liquid fat. If time allows, a much easier and more effective way of removing all fat is to allow the stock to become quite cold so that the fat hardens into a solid surface layer and can then be lifted off quite easily with a knife.

Final straining and flavouring
After de-greasing, strain stock again, this time through a colander lined with butter muslin, to remove any impurities and small particles of meat or vegetables which may have slipped through during initial straining, otherwise the stock may quickly sour. Reheat the stock and, if flavouring is too weak for your purposes, boil over high heat to evaporate some of the liquid and to concentrate flavour. Correct seasoning, if necessary, by adding salt and pepper.

STORING STOCKS
Meat stock can be covered and kept in a refrigerator for up to 10 days but

1 Cut vegetables into chunks. Put in a heavy pan with washed meat or fish bones.

5 Half cover the pan and simmer for as long as specified in the recipe used.

OR cool stock a little then skim off fat with a skimmer or spoon.

Step-by-step white stock

2 Add cold water to the pan and bring to the boil as slowly as possible.

3 When the thick foam forms into a definite scum, remove with a spoon or skimmer.

4 When the scum has stopped rising in large quantities, add herbs and seasonings.

6 Skim and top up with boiling water if the liquid falls below the level of the ingredients.

7 Pour the stock through a colander into a clean bowl or pan. Reserve ingredients.

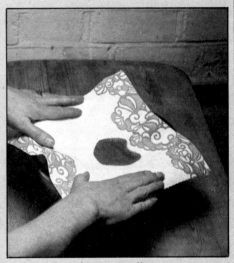

8 If stock is for immediate use, mop up fat with kitchen paper or a slice of bread.

OR leave until completely cold, then scrape off solid fat.

9 Strain de-greased stock through a sieve lined with fine muslin or cheesecloth.

10 Reheat. If the flavouring is weak, boil rapidly to reduce and concentrate flavour. Season to taste.

it should be boiled up every 3 – 4 days to keep it sweet. Fish stock should be used (or frozen) within 24 hours. Vegetable stock will keep for a maximum of 3 days but must be boiled up daily.

All stocks freeze well but they are bulky so it is a good idea to reduce your stock more than usual, concentrating its flavour well before freezing. You can always dilute it again. Pour into ice cube trays, calculating the number of cubes per 150 ml [¼ pt], and freeze. When frozen, turn into plastic bags and label. Frozen meat stock will keep for two months, frozen fish and vegetable stock for 1 month.

BROWN STOCK

This is the ideal stock to use in dishes which require a good colour and strong flavour. If you cannot find Spanish onions, very large, well-flavoured onions will do.

MAKES ABOUT 1.25 L [3 pt]
2.25 kg [5 lb] shin or neck beef bones with meat attached, chopped and washed
2 Spanish onions, sliced
3 large carrots, chopped
2 celery stalks, thickly sliced
salt
bouquet garni
bay leaf
6 black peppercorns

1 Put the bones in a large pan, extract fat and fry for 15 minutes, stirring occasionally, to brown bones evenly. Add a little dripping if necessary.

2 Add the prepared vegetables and cook gently until just coloured.

3 Pour on 3.25 L [6 pt] cold water and bring slowly to the boil.

4 Remove scum with a slotted spoon.

5 Add a little salt, the herbs and the peppercorns. Half cover the pan and simmer very gently for about 4 hours, skimming and topping up with boiling water as necessary.

6 Strain, de-grease, strain again, reduce and adjust seasoning to taste as necessary.

Variations
● Second brown stock: brown stock

Step-by-step brown stock

1 Cook the washed bones in a large pan over very low heat until fat is extracted.

2 Slightly increase heat and fry for 15 mins. Stir to brown evenly. Add a little fat if bones produce none.

3 Meanwhile, prepare the vegetables: peel and slice onions, scrub carrots and celery and then cut them into chunks.

4 Add vegetables to the pan and cook for 10 minutes or until pale golden in colour. Continue from step 2 of white stock (see below).

bones and meat can be re-used. To bolster flavour, add fresh vegetables and herbs and any joint bones and any chicken carcasses saved.
● Cheap brown stock: you can simply use saved joint bones and chicken carcasses in place of fresh shin or neck of beef bones. Reduce water by half.

WHITE STOCK

White stock, with its more delicate flavour, is the perfect base for cream soups and special sauces.

MAKES ABOUT 1.25 L [3 pt]
2.25 kg [5 lb] knuckle of veal, chopped and blanched
2 Spanish onions, sliced
3 large carrots, chopped
2 celery stalks, thickly sliced
1 medium-sized leek, thickly sliced
salt
6 white peppercorns
bouquet garni

1 Blanch the bones by plunging into boiling water for 5 minutes. Rinse in cold water.

2 Put the blanched bones in a large pan. Add vegetables, pour on to it 3.25 L [6 pt] cold water and bring to the boil slowly.

3 Remove scum with a slotted spoon.

4 Add salt, peppercorns and herbs and bring back to the boil.

5 Reduce heat, half cover the pan and simmer very gently for about 4 hours, skimming and topping up with boiling water as necessary.

6 Strain, de-grease, strain again, reduce and adjust seasoning to taste as necessary.

Variations
● Second white stock: bones used for white stock can be re-used with fresh vegetables and herbs. Add a chicken carcass to bolster flavour.

- Cheap white stock: replace fresh veal knuckle with leftover veal, chicken, beef or rabbit bones, or a mixture of all of these. Leftover pork, lamb or mutton bones can also be included but they must form only a very small proportion of the total bones if you want to make a general-purpose white stock.

HOUSEHOLD STOCK

▽▽▽△△△ *Based on leftovers, this stock is very economic to make. Use it for casseroles, broths and other dishes which do not require a strongly coloured or flavoured stock. You could use a cooked joint bone, the carcass of a cooked bird, raw bones, cooked or raw meat trimmings, giblets, bacon rinds. But do not include too many different types of meat or bones or the flavours will cancel each other out. Be sure that cooked bones have not begun to develop 'off' flavours.*

MAKES ABOUT 1.25 L [3 pt]
**2.25 kg [5 lb] selection of bones and meat trimmings
2 large onions, peeled and sliced
1 carrot, sliced
1 leek, cleaned and sliced
2 celery stalks, thickly sliced
bouquet garni
6 black peppercorns
salt**

1 Chop the bones into convenient-sized pieces.

2 Add the vegetables.

3 Pour on 3.25 L [6 pt] cold water and bring slowly to the boil.

4 Remove scum with a slotted spoon.

5 Add a little salt, the herbs and the peppercorns. Half cover the pan and simmer very gently for about 3 hours, skimming and topping up with boiling water as necessary.

6 Strain, de-grease, strain again, reduce and adjust seasoning to taste as required.

Variations
● Brown household stock: to give the stock extra colour, fry the bones for 15 minutes, stirring occasionally, to brown evenly. Add extra fat if necessary. Then continue from step 2 of household stock.

CHICKEN STOCK

▽▽▽△△△ *This is one of the most useful of all stocks, frequently specified in recipes.*

MAKES 1.25 L [3 pt]
**1.40–1.60 kg [3–3½ lb] boiling fowl
700 g [1½ lb] knuckle of veal, chopped and blanched
2 large carrots, cut into quarters
2 Spanish onions, cut into quarters
1 leek, thickly sliced
1 celery stick, sliced
bouquet garni
6 white peppercorns
salt**

1 Put the chicken, giblets (excluding liver) and veal in a large pan. Add vegetables, pour on 3.25 L [6 pt] water and bring slowly to the boil.

2 Remove scum with a slotted spoon.

3 Add bouquet garni, pepper and a little salt and bring back to the boil.

4 Reduce heat, half cover the pan and simmer very gently for 2½–3 hours until the meat falls away from the bone. Skim and top up with boiling water if the level of the liquid falls below the top of ingredients.

5 Strain, de-grease, reduce, strain again, and adjust seasoning to taste.

Variations
● Second chicken stock: re-use the carcass with fresh vegetables (1 carrot, 1 leek, 1 onion, 50 g [2 oz] mushroom stalks or peelings), herbs and 1.40 L [2½ pt] water to make a second stock.
● Giblet stock: wash the liver, gizzard and heart. Wash and scald the feet if you have them, scrape away the scales and nip off claws with pliers. Put everything in a saucepan together with a piece of celery, half an onion and a bouquet garni. Stew gently for ¾–1 hour. Strain, de-grease and use for gravies or soups.

GAME STOCK

▽▽▽△△△ *Use pheasant, partridge, pigeon or any other game carcass to accompany game dishes. If bones weigh less than the amount specified here, just reduce the amount of water you use.*

MAKES 850 ml [1½ pt]
**700 g [1½ lb] game carcasses
1 small onion, cut into quarters
1 carrot, cut into quarters
1 celery stick, sliced
parsley sprig
bouquet garni
4 black peppercorns
salt
1 L [2 pt] second brown stock (see page 58).**

1 Break up carcasses, put into a large pan and just cover with cold water. Leave for 1 hour. Add vegetables.

2 Bring slowly to the boil and remove scum with a slotted spoon.

3 Add herbs, pepper, salt and stock and bring back to the boil.

4 Reduce heat, half cover the pan and simmer very gently for 2 hours or until all flesh has separated from the bones.

5 Strain, de-grease, strain again, reduce and adjust seasoning to taste.

FISH STOCK

▽△ *This is exceptionally quick to make. The reason for the short cooking time is that the fish bones and trimmings give up their flavour much faster than meat bones. Simmer for no longer than 30 minutes or the bones will give the stock a bitter, gluey flavour. Any non-oily white fish trimmings can be used but the inclusion of a halibut or turbot head produces the best stock. Always use fish stock within 24 hours.*

MAKES ½ L [1 pt]
**675 g (1½ lb) white fish trimmings
1 medium-sized onion or leek, sliced
1 celery stalk, sliced
juice of half a lemon
a few parsley stalks
small bouquet garni
6 white peppercorns
salt**

1 Wash the fish trimmings well under cold running water. Put in a

large pan, add vegetables, cover with 1 L [2 pt] cold water and bring slowly to the boil.

2 Remove scum with a slotted spoon.

3 Add remaining ingredients, bring back to the boil, half cover with a lid and leave to simmer for 20–30 minutes.

4 Strain the stock into another saucepan through a sieve lined with butter muslin or cheesecloth. Press the bones with the back of a wooden spoon to extract all the juices, then discard the bones.

5 Boil the strained stock over high heat until it has been reduced by half and the flavour has been concentrated.

6 Adjust the seasoning and use immediately, or freeze when cold.

VEGETABLE STOCK

Here is an excellent way to use up vegetable peelings and scraps. Avoid using too much of strongly flavoured vegetables such as cabbage and greens as these will overpower the delicate flavour of the stock.

MAKES 850 ml (1½ pt]

350 g [¾ lb] vegetable peelings, such as outer stalks of celery, watercress stalks, carrot peelings, tomato and mushroom peelings and stalks, green parts of leeks
3 white peppercorns
small bouquet garni
salt

1 Rinse the peelings under cold running water. Put them in a pan, add the peppercorns, bouquet garni and salt, 1.15 L [2 pt] cold water and bring to the boil.

2 Reduce heat, half cover with a lid and leave to simmer gently for 1–1½ hours.

3 Strain, reduce and adjust seasoning to taste.

Variation

● Brown vegetable stock: vegetables can be browned by frying in butter before you add the water. The sweetness in the vegetables will caramelize, adding flavour and colour.

MAKING THIN SOUPS

The simplest way to use stock is to make thin soups. These are made by cooking ingredients in stock. The liquid is not thickened except where one of the ingredients does this naturally (as when a potato disintegrates into the soup).

A really well-flavoured stock is essential to a thin soup because cooking time is usually very short (often only a few minutes), so the added ingredients do not have much chance to impart their flavour to the liquid. Brown, white, chicken and fish stocks are all suitable for making thin soups, and first stocks with their finer flavour are best.

AVGOLEMONO

Any white stock (chicken or veal) can be used. Leftover cooked rice can also be used – add it to the pan at the last minute, giving it just enough time to warm through.

This soup can be eaten either hot or cold. Served hot it has a very delicate flavour; served cold the taste is more lemony. If served cold, add a touch of elegance by garnishing with paper-thin slices of lemon and sprigs of dill weed.

SERVES 4 – 6
1.15 L [2 pt] white stock
50 g [2 oz] long-grain rice
3 eggs
juice of 2 small lemons
freshly ground black pepper

1 Bring the stock to the boil.

2 Sprinkle in the rice and simmer gently for about 15 minutes or until the rice is tender. To test this, fish out a grain of rice and bite it. If it is still hard, further cooking is required.

3 Meanwhile, break the eggs into a bowl, add the lemon juice and beat (stir vigorously) with a fork.

4 When the rice is cooked, remove the pan from the heat.

Home-made stocks are satisfying to make and not too taxing on the cook. Meat stocks do require long cooking but this can be stopped and started again as suits you. Pictured just before straining are: Top left, subtly flavoured chicken stock; Bottom left, quickly-cooked fish stock; Right, rich and beefy brown stock.

5 Stir a ladleful of hot stock into the egg mixture.

6 Add the egg mixture to the pan of stock, whisking in with a rotary or balloon whisk.

7 Reheat soup over low heat, stirring gently until it is the consistency of thin cream. Do not allow the soup to boil or the eggs will scramble.

8 Season and serve.

TASTY CHICKEN AND MUSHROOM SOUP

⧖*Dried Chinese mushrooms which are available from Chinese supermarkets are best for this soup as they have a strong, distinctive flavour. If dried are unobtainable use sliced fresh mushrooms instead.*

SERVES 4–6
1.15 L [2 pt] chicken stock
50 g [2 oz] dried sliced Chinese mushrooms or 4 button mushrooms thinly sliced
125 g [5 oz] cooked chicken breast
salt
freshly ground black pepper
sprigs of watercress to garnish

1 Reconstitute the dried mushrooms by soaking in hot water for 20 minutes or until swollen.

2 Skin the chicken breast and cut into slivers.

3 Bring the stock to the boil. Add the

Chicken stock is the basis for this Chinese-style chicken and mushroom soup.

drained mushrooms and chicken.

4 Simmer for 5 minutes. Season to taste and garnish with watercress.

Variations

● For a luxurious version of chicken and mushroom soup, add 60 ml [4 tablespoons] of dry sherry just before serving.

● Instead of chicken meat use turkey or pork. Just before the end of cooking, add a few slices of cucumber.

STRACCIATELLA

⧖*It is essential to stir while adding the egg or it will set in a solid lump rather than being dispersed in fine threads (or rags, to give the literal Italian translation). Serve immediately or the egg will overcook and become rubbery in texture.*

SERVES 4–6
1.15 L [2 pt] chicken stock
30 ml [2 tablespoons] grated Parmesan cheese
2 eggs

1 Break the eggs into a bowl. Add the cheese and beat (stir vigorously) with a fork until well blended.

2 Bring the stock to the boil over medium heat.

3 As soon as the stock reaches boil-

ing point, add the egg and cheese, pouring in a thin stream and stirring the stock vigorously to break the egg into strands.

4 Remove from heat and serve immediately.

HOT AND SOUR SOUP

⧖*Because this soup is Chinese in origin many of the ingredients are rather exotic. If you are unable to obtain bamboo shoots, use a small can of drained asparagus tips instead. Ordinary open mushrooms can be used instead of the dried Chinese kind and, sunflower oil can be substituted for sesame oil.*

SERVES 4
850 ml [1½ pt] beef stock
50 g [2 oz] dried sliced Chinese mushrooms or 4 fresh mushrooms sliced
30 ml [1 tablespoon] soy sauce
2.5 ml [½ teaspoon] chilli sauce
salt
freshly ground black pepper
100 g [¼ lb] rump steak
100g [4 oz] canned bamboo shoots
4 spring onions
30 ml [1 tablespoon] dry sherry

1 Soak the mushrooms in hot water for 20 minutes. Drain and discard the liquid.

2 Bring the stock to the boil. Add the soy sauce, chilli sauce, salt and pepper. Remove from heat.

3 Using a sharp knife, cut the meat into very thin strips.

4 Drain the bamboo shoots and cut into small pieces.

5 Trim the spring onions and cut in half.

6 Return the stock to the heat and bring back to the boil.

7 Add the meat, reduce heat and simmer for 5 minutes.

8 Add the bamboo shoots and onions and simmer for a further 4 minutes.

9 Remove from heat, stir in the sherry and serve immediately.

Soups

hearty soups

A meal cooked using only one pan and served in the dish in which it was cooked has an obvious advantage when it comes to washing up. Meal-in-a-bowl soups are easy and economic to make; and they are hot, tasty and filling—ideal family fare on a cold day.

There are two types of hearty soups. The end result is much the same in both cases, really a cross between a soup and a stew comprising a thin but richly-flavoured liquid filled with meat, vegetables and other delicious ingredients of your choice.

There is only one major difference between the two types of soup—the cooking time. Broths are based on meaty bones and water, so long simmering is essential to extract maximum flavour from the meat to produce a tasty liquid. The liquid element in stock-based soup is, of course, very tasty right from the start, so cooking time is relatively brief – just long enough to cook the ingredients that are served in it.

The liquid is not thickened with flour, cream or eggs in either broths or stock-based soups, but some of the ingredients (such as potato) may disintegrate during cooking and thus thicken the liquid a little. The soups are made substantial by the inclusion of the many solid ingredients which are cooked and served in it. You can use all sorts of vegetables, pulses (dried peas, beans and lentils), pasta, rice, barley, tapioca, meat (including sliced Frankfurters and other sausages), cheese and even poached eggs. These soups are, therefore, an excellent and economic way of using up leftovers or quantities of fresh food too small to make a dish on their own.

These hearty soups are excellent for inexpensive family meals, particularly if they are served with crusty bread and butter. They are so filling that all you need serve afterwards is cheese and a salad or fruit. You can also adapt these soups for the first course of a meal: for the same number of people, use the quantity of bones and liquid specified in a recipe but reduce the other ingredients by half to make the soup slightly less substantial.

BROTHS
Although broths require long slow cooking, they need comparatively little attention from the cook so they are a good dish to make when you plan to spend an afternoon in the kitchen doing other jobs such as making pastry or on wash day.

It is important to choose bones with a high proportion of meat attached to them in order to flavour the liquid well and provide chunks of meat to eat in the final dish. Rinse the bones quickly under a cold running tap to wash away any dirt or scum. Then cut away and discard (or render down) as much fat as possible.

The vegetables used in broths should always be fresh. Trim and chop them finely and add them to the pan near the beginning of cooking time.

Cut surfaces and lengthy cooking time do not matter when making broths because, although these factors inevitably mean that flavour and nutrients will escape from the

Minestrone, based on home-made beef stock, is rich and nourishing.

11

ingredients themselves, they are trapped in the liquid.

Cereals, pulses and pasta, if used, are cooked in the broth only for as long as is needed to make them tender. There is no point in adding them to the pan any earlier because, unlike meat and vegetables, they do not add any flavour to the liquid—they only increase the bulk of the final dish.

Broths, like stocks, should be meticulously skimmed during the early stages of cooking and any fat that floats to the surface should be removed before serving. This is particularly important when a fatty cut of meat, such as mutton scrag, is used or the final dish will be unpleasantly oily.

Broths are not strained before serving. They are served complete with all the ingredients that went into their making—except, of course, the bones. Lift the bones out when the broth is cooked, and discard them (or save for making a second stock) after removing the meat. The meat should be well cooked after long simmering and fall easily from the bone. Cut the meat into bite-sized pieces, discarding any gristle, fat or skin that might be attached. Return the meat to the pan and reheat gently before serving.

STOCK-BASED SOUPS

These soups are very simple and comparatively quick to prepare: cooking time is determined by how long it takes to tenderize the hardest ingredient. The choice of ingredients is almost limitless and includes left-over cooked foods as well as fresh ones. But for really tasty results two things are essential. First, the stock must be really well flavoured (and that means a good home-made stock as described in the last chapter. Secondly, the ingredients must be added to the pan in the right order and at suitable intervals so that everything is tender, hot and ready to serve at the same time. Those requiring the longest cooking time, such as pulses, must be added right from the start. Add hard root vegetables next, cut into 2.5 cm [1"] dice, then pasta or rice, followed by the softer fresh vegetables, again cut into 2.5 cm [1"] dice, and, finally, any cooked ingredients (such as left-over vegetables, bite-sized pieces of meat and slices of sausage) which simply need heating through.

Step-by-step broth

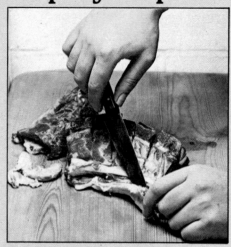

1 Rinse bones under cold running water. Using a sharp knife cut away as much fat as possible.

2 Put the meaty bones in a large flameproof casserole or saucepan and cover with cold water.

4 Add salt (and barley if used), cover the pan with a lid and simmer gently for 30 minutes.

5 Thoroughly scrub or peel the vegetables and cut them into dice about 2.5 cm [1"] square.

7 Turn off heat. Lift bones from the pan and discard after removing meat. Cut the meat into pieces.

8 Float kitchen paper or a slice of bread on the surface of the broth to mop up liquid surface fat.

3 Bring slowly to the boil. Using a flat skimmer, remove scum and rising fat as it forms.

6 Add the vegetables to the pan and continue simmering, covered, for a further 1½ hours.

9 Put bite-sized pieces of meat into the pan and gently reheat the broth. Garnish and serve.

SCOTCH BROTH

Here is a traditional and very popular broth. The secret for success lies in removing as much of the fat as possible from the meat, both before and after cooking. Cook and serve Scotch broth straight from the saucepan or, if you wish to take the dish to the table, in a large flameproof casserole.

SERVES 6
700 g [1½ lb] mutton scrag
    or middle neck of lamb
5 ml [1 teaspoon] salt
40 g [1½ oz] pearl barley
3 small carrots
3 small leeks
2 small turnips
1 onion
2 celery stalks
freshly ground black pepper
15 ml [1 tablespoon]
    parsley

1 Rinse the meaty bones under a cold running tap and shake to drain.

2 Cut away as much fat as possible and discard. Chop the bones, if the butcher has not done this, so they will fit into your pan.

3 Put the bones into the pan and cover with 1.7 L [3 pt] cold water.

4 Bring slowly to the boil. When scum and surface fat form, skim them away with a flat skimmer or perforated spoon. Skim for several minutes as the fat rises.

5 When all the scum has been removed, add the salt and barley. Cover the pan with the lid and simmer for 30 minutes.

6 Prepare the vegetables by scrubbing or peeling. Chop them into 2.5 cm [1"] dice.

7 Add the vegetables and cover the pan with a lid and continue simmering for a further 1½ hours.

8 When the broth is cooked, turn off heat and lift the bones on to a plate, using a perforated spoon.

9 Using a fork, detach the meat from the bones and shred or cut it into bite-sized pieces. Discard bones and any fat or gristle.

10 Remove as much surface fat as possible from the broth, mopping it up with absorbent kitchen paper or slices of bread.

11 Return the meat to the pan. Reheat gently and adjust seasoning to taste.

12 Sprinkle the broth with chopped parsley just before serving.

COCK-A-LEEKIE

This is another substantial Scottish soup suitable for a family meal. Not all the chicken meat is used in the final soup. After cooking, breast meat can be saved and used for a salad or another dish. For maximum economy, a small proportion – about 75 g [3 oz] – of chicken skin can be included in the soup, but only use the thinnest and whitest skin and chop it into strips smaller than a matchstick. Prunes are traditionally served in the dish and add an unusual element to a white soup. Include some of the green part of the leeks to add welcome colour to this soup.

SERVES 6
1.8 kg [4 lb] boiling fowl
12 large prunes
1.4 kg [3 lb] leeks
2 celery stalks
bouquet garni
salt and pepper

1 Put the prunes in a small saucepan. Cover with cold water and bring to the boil.

2 Remove the pan from the heat, cover with a lid and set aside until cold.

3 Place the chicken in a large flameproof casserole or saucepan and add 2.2 L [4 pt] cold water. Use more water if necessary because the chicken should be completely covered.

4 Place the pan over a moderately high heat and bring to boil.

5 Using a flat skimmer or perforated spoon, skim off any scum that rises to the surface.

6 Reduce heat, cover the pan with a well-fitting lid and simmer for an hour.

13

Herb dumplings in beef broth make an economical and filling meal-in-a-bowl. Oxtail broth, served without the meat, is an economical soup.

7 Meanwhile, wash and prepare the vegetables. Retaining 5 cm [2″] of the green stem, cut the leeks into 2.5 cm [1″] lengths. Cut the celery into 12 mm [½″] lengths.

8 When the hour is up, add the vegetables and bouquet garni to the pan.

9 Half cover the pan with a lid and simmer for a further 50 minutes.

10 Drain the prunes, slit them open and discard stones.

11 Add the prunes to the pan. Half cover it with the lid and continue simmering for 10 minutes or until the chicken is well cooked and falls easily from the bones. You can test this by lifting the chicken from the pan. If a leg joint is easily pulled off the body, the chicken is ready and will be easy to dismember.

12 Turn the heat off and lift the chicken out of the pan on to a plate.

13 When the chicken has cooled a little, skin and dismember it using your hands.

14 Discard the bones and all the skin except the best-looking bit over the breast.

15 Set the breast meat aside to use in another dish, and the leg meat, too, if you wish.

16 Cut the remaining pieces of meat into bite-sized pieces.

17 Roll the breast skin tightly and cut into thin slivers with scissors.

18 Using absorbent kitchen paper or a slice of bread, remove surface fat from the soup. Remove and discard the bouquet garni.

19 Add the bite-sized pieces of chicken and slivers of breast skin to the pan.

20 Reheat gently. Check seasoning and serve.

Making croûtons

Crispy cubes of freshly fried bread floated on the top of the soup as it is served make it look more attractive and add crunchy texture. Home-made croûtons are very much nicer than any cracker or soup-sprinkle that you can buy – and they are much more economical.

Stale bread makes better croûtons than fresh bread and this is a good use for the ends of loaves. Three or four thick slices will make enough croûtons for four people.

Fry the croûtons in shallow fat until golden, then drain them thoroughly on kitchen paper. Serve immediately or keep warm in a low oven until required.

You will need about 50 g [2 oz] of fat to fry croûtons made from four slices of bread. If you have sufficient quantity of bacon dripping this will give the croûtons a lovely flavour. Other suitable fats are butter (add 5 ml [1 teaspoon] of oil to prevent the butter from burning) and tasteless vegetable oil.

Plain, unflavoured croûtons are always popular but you can flavour them if you wish.

Make a garlic paste by chopping a clove of garlic finely, then mashing it in 5 ml [1 teaspoon] of salt with the edge of a round-bladed knife. Work in 15 ml [1 tablespoon] of butter to make sufficient paste to spread on four slices.

Commercial anchovy paste can be used in place of garlic salt and butter but it must be spread thinly or flavour will be overpowering. Fish-flavoured croûtons are not suitable for all soups.

OXTAIL BROTH

▨▨▨ *In this recipe vegetables and* ▲▲▲ *meat are gently fried in oil before the water is added. This gives the broth extra flavour and a rich brown colour. Because oxtail is inclined to be very fatty it is important to remove as much fat as possible after cooking. It is therefore best to chill the broth completely so that all the fat solidifies and can be lifted off the soup.*

SERVES 4
1 oxtail, weighing about 700 g [1½ lb]
1 large onion
1 small turnip
1 celery stalk
2 cloves
15 ml [1 tablespoon] vegetable oil
salt
6 peppercorns
1 bay leaf
2 small carrots
15 ml [1 tablespoon] parsley

1 Rinse the oxtail under cold running water and shake dry. Using a sharp knife, divide it into joints and remove fat.

2 Scrub the vegetables, halve the onion and turnip and chop the celery into four pieces. Stud the onion with the cloves.

3 Warm the oil in a large flameproof casserole or saucepan over medium heat.

4 When the oil is hot add the vegetables and fry, turning, until lightly browned all over.

5 Add the oxtail pieces to the pan and fry until browned.

6 Pour on 1.15 L [2 pt] cold water and bring to the boil.

7 Remove scum and fat with a skimmer or perforated spoon.

8 Reduce heat and add some salt,

1 Spread the flavouring, if used, on four thick slices of bread.

2 Pile up the slices and remove the crusts.

3 Cut the crustless bread into cubes and set aside.

4 When the fat is hot add the croûtons, spread in a single layer.

5 Fry for about 2 minutes, turning to brown on all sides.

6 Lift out of the pan and thoroughly drain on kitchen paper.

peppercorns and bay leaf. Cover pan with a well-fitting lid and simmer gently for 3 hours.

9 Strain the broth through a colander into a large bowl. Discard the vegetables and seasonings and transfer the bones to a plate.

10 Using a fork or knife, remove the meat from the bones. Discard bones, fat and any gristle.

11 Reserve half the meat for another dish. Cut the remainder into bite-sized pieces.

12 When the shreds of meat are cold, put them into a rigid airtight container and refrigerate until required.

13 Cover the broth when cool and refrigerate for 8 hours or overnight.

14 Lift the cold fat from the surface of the broth and discard. Turn the broth into a pan and reheat gently.

15 Peel and trim the carrots and cut them into matchstick-sized pieces (called julienne strips).

16 Add the shreds of meat and julienne strips to the pan and cook for 3-4 minutes.

17 Chop the parsley and garnish the broth before serving.

BEEF SOUP WITH HERB DUMPLINGS

The addition of home-made dumplings makes this a very filling meal-in-a-bowl for a cold day. The dumplings shown here are beautifully light because breadcrumbs are used in place of some of the flour. In order to bind (hold together) the breadcrumbs thoroughly into the pastry, egg is used instead of water.

Make 4-5 small ones or one large one for each person. Add 20 minutes to the cooking time for larger ones.

Add shreds of meat reserved after making the broth or from leftovers.

SERVES 6
1.15 L [2 pt] beef stock
125 g [¼ lb] cooked beef cut into bite-sized pieces
75 g [3 oz] onion
75 g [3 oz] carrot

50 g [2 oz] potato
1 celery stalk
salt and pepper

For the dumplings:
50 g [2 oz] self-raising flour
50 g [2 oz] fresh breadcrumbs
50 g [2 oz] shredded suet
15 ml [1 tablespoon] freshly chopped mixed herbs
1 small egg
salt and pepper

1 Make the suet pastry for the dumplings by the usual method. adding the herbs and breadcrumbs with the dry ingredients. Beat the egg with a fork and add it in place of the usual water.

2 Put the dough on to a floured board. Divide it into pieces smaller than a walnut and roll each piece into a ball between your floured palms.

3 Put the beef stock into a flameproof casserole or saucepan and bring to simmering point.

4 Scrub or peel and trim the vegetables. Chop the onions, dice the carrots and potatoes, and slice the celery. Add to the pan and simmer for 5 minutes.

5 Add the dumplings, cover the pan with a lid and simmer for a further 10 minutes.

6 Two or three minutes before the end of cooking time, add the meat in shreds. Then check seasoning.

MINESTRONE

Pulses (dried peas, beans and lentils) must be soaked overnight and partially cooked before adding to the soup because they take so long to tenderize. Never cook pulses with salt because it hardens their skins; add salt only to the final dish just before serving.

When serving the soup, pass round a small bowl of grated Parmesan cheese so that each person can sprinkle more cheese on top of his soup. Offer diners croûtons, too, if you wish.

SERVES 6
50 g [2 oz] dried haricot beans
2 rashers bacon
1 clove garlic
1 medium-sized onion

3 tomatoes
1 large carrot
1 celery stalk
1.15 L [2 pt] beef or chicken stock
50 g [2 oz] pasta shapes
30 ml [2 tablespoons] Parmesan cheese
salt and pepper

1 Put the beans in a large bowl. Cover them with plenty of cold water and leave to soak overnight.

2 Drain the beans. Put them into a pan with fresh cold water and bring to the boil. Cover and simmer for 1 hour.

3 Chop the bacon into matchstick-sized pieces and put into a large flameproof casserole or saucepan. Place over low heat and cook until the fat starts to run.

4 Prepare the vegetables. Chop the garlic finely and cut the onion into thin slices.

5 Add the garlic and onion to the pan, cover and allow them to soften without colouring (this is called sweating). Shake the pan occasionally or stir to prevent sticking.

6 Add the stock to the pan, increase heat and bring to the boil.

7 Quarter the tomatoes and dice the other vegetables.

8 Add the carrots and drained, partly cooked beans. Reduce heat, cover the pan and simmer for 20 minutes.

9 Add the celery and tomatoes and continue simmering for a further 10 minutes.

10 Then bring the soup back to the boil and add the pasta shapes. Lower the heat and simmer until they are soft. The timing will depend on the size of the pasta – be guided by the packet instructions. For small shapes 8 minutes should be enough, for larger ones 12 minutes.

11 Stir in 30 ml [2 tablespoons] Parmesan cheese, season to taste with salt and freshly ground pepper and serve.

Moules à la marinière

Moules à la marinière

Shellfish add a touch of luxury to any meal; mussels are a great treat and fortunately they do not cost a great deal—rather the reverse.

This dish comes from France's Atlantic coast and is excellent, providing that the mussels are fresh and thoroughly cleaned. Gritty mussels are unpleasant to eat, while sand left in the soup will collect in the liquor, turning it grey. Dead mussels can give you nasty food poisoning, so be sure that they are alive, by the means described here.

Serve moules à la marinière as a meal-in-a-bowl for two people or a first course for four. For a meal-in-a-bowl buy 1 kg [2¼ lb] of mussels per person if sold by weight, or 1 L [1 qt] if sold by volume.

If a large number of mussels in the fishmonger's tray are open or the shells are broken, do not buy them because these will be dead. (Live mussels usually keep their shells closed when they are out of water.)

When you get home, clean the mussels thoroughly. This is not difficult but it does take time. Keep the cleaned mussels immersed in a bowl of water until required for cooking, changing the water several times.

Eat mussels on the day of purchase whenever possible. If you have to leave them overnight, add some salt to the water. If wished you can add a little flour or oatmeal, too, to feed the mussels so they become plump and white. Cover the bowl with a clean cloth and put in a cool place.

After cooking, check again that your mussels are fresh. Heat should force the shells open so discard any that remain closed.

It is usual to remove half the shell from each mussel before serving. This is to reduce the amount of shell in the soup bowls. Put an empty plate in the centre of the table for the remaining halves of the shells as each person discards them.

Serve in soup bowls with the mussels piled up, and provide spoons for the soup liquid. To eat the mussels, you pick the shell up in your fingers and tip the mussel into your mouth, discarding the empty shell. It is therefore a good idea to provide big napkins to wipe sticky fingers, and finger-bowls would also be useful.

SERVES 2
2 kg [2 quarts] mussels
1 onion
1 shallot (or a second onion)
1 garlic clove
4 parsley stalks
thyme sprig or dried thyme
salt and pepper
40 g [1½ oz] butter
200 ml [7 fl oz] dry white wine
  or dry cider
75 ml [3 fl oz] water
15 ml [1 tablespoon] chopped
  parsley

1 Mussels should be absolutely fresh. Tap any open mussel. Discard it if it does not shut.

5 When ready to cook, drain the mussels. Chop the garlic, onion and shallot very finely.

6 Melt butter in a large saucepan over low heat. Add vegetables, cover and sweat for 10 minutes.

10 Reduce the heat and cook for a further 3 minutes to make sure the mussels are cooked.

11 Strain the liquor through a colander into a second saucepan. Discard the herbs.

2 Using your hands, pull away beards (any hanging seaweed gripped between the two shells).

3 Scrub the mussels under cold running water. Scrape away encrustations with a sharp knife.

4 Keep the mussels in a bowl of cold water until ready to cook. Change the water several times.

7 Tie parsley stalks and thyme with a piece of fine string. Or tie up dried thyme in buttermuslin.

8 Add the herbs, wine or cider and water to the pan. Heat through slowly until almost boiling.

9 Add the mussels, cover and shake gently over fierce heat for 2 minutes to open the shells.

12 Discard any mussels that are still tightly shut. Remove half a shell from each that is open.

13 Add the mussels on their half shells to the liquor in the pan. Reheat gently and season to taste.

14 Ladle soup into a tureen or bowls, heaping up the mussels in the centre. Garnish with parsley.

French onion soup makes an economical and satisfying start to the meal.

French onion soup

◩◩ This classic soup is unusual because it introduces cheese at the beginning of the meal. Serve the soup in a large oven proof tureen or six individual oven proof bowls, each topped with an island of sizzling toasted cheese. Each person submerges his own cheese island under the soup as he eats it, pressing the bread against the bottom of the bowl with the edge of a soup spoon to cut it into bite-sized pieces. If you do not have time to make beef stock, you could use canned consommé. For an extra rich soup add 15 ml [1 tablespoon] of brandy per serving. Stir in the brandy just before the end of cooking.

SERVES 6
350 g [¾ lb] onions
75 g [3 oz] margarine
1 L [2 pt] well-flavoured beef stock
bay leaf
salt and pepper
6 thick slices of French bread
100 g [¼ lb] Emmenthal cheese
30 ml [2 tablespoons] Parmesan cheese

1 Skin and finely chop the onions.

2 Melt the margarine in a heavy-based pan. Add the onions and cook over a low heat, stirring occasionally, until browned.

3 Add the stock and bay leaf. Season with salt and pepper. Cover pan and simmer gently for 30 minutes.

4 Grate the Emmenthal cheese, put it in a bowl, add the Parmesan cheese and mix the two together.

5 Heat the grill and heat the oven to 200°C [400°F] gas mark 6.

6 Toast the bread lightly on each side.

7 Remove the bay leaf and pour the soup into an oven proof soup tureen or six individual bowls.

8 Cover each slice of bread with cheese and float the bread on top of the soup.

9 Carefully put the soup tureen or bowls into the oven and cook for 10–15 minutes, or until the cheese is melted and sizzling.

Green pea and bacon soup

Serve this hearty soup with crisp French bread.

Dried green peas are very hard when they are bought so they must be soaked overnight before they can be used. Green peas are available either whole or split. Both can be used to make this soup.

You can use 75 g [3 oz] diced cooked ham instead of bacon rashers. Add it at step 9.

If you make the soup in advance, up to step 8 in the recipe, it will keep, covered, in the refrigerator for 3 days. It will not keep quite so long after the milk has been added so if you have any soup left over, eat it within 2 days.

SERVES 6
200 g [7 oz] dried green peas
1.7 L [3 pt] ham or bacon
**   stock**
1 large onion
1 small carrot
a small piece of turnip
4 bacon rashers
50 g [2 oz] butter
bouquet garni
150 ml [¼ pt] milk

1 Soak the dried peas in water for at least 8 hours or overnight. The water must be cold and must cover the peas.

2 Peel and chop the onion into small pieces.

3 Scrub and chop the carrot. Peel and chop the turnip.

4 Remove and discard bacon rind.

Cut bacon into small pieces using kitchen scissors.

5 Melt the butter in a large heavy-based saucepan over low heat. Do not allow it to brown.

6 Add the bacon and chopped vegetables. Cook until the bacon and onion are just transparent.

7 Drain any surplus water off the peas and add to the pan with the stock and bouquet garni. Bring to the boil and cover.

8 Simmer over low heat for 2-2½ hours until the vegetables are reduced to a pulp.

9 Just before serving, remove the bouquet garni, check seasoning, add cooked ham if used, stir in the milk and reheat if necessary.

Soups

purée soups

For generous flavour, nourishment, good texture and simplicity of method, purée soups are a beginner's delight. You will find the inviting smells and superb flavour of a home-made soup tremendously satisfying.

Creamy vegetable purée soups are amazingly quick to make, and really economical too. A soup tureen makes an excellent investment for the shoestring cook – guests will be lured to the dining table by warm, inviting smells, and the delicious taste of a simple soup is so utterly different from canned products, as well as being really wholesome and nourishing. Purée soups make a very satisfying start to a meal, and the simple addition of swirls of cream or a garnish, such as crisply fried golden croûtons, will turn a simple soup into real dinner party fare.

VEGETABLE PUREE SOUPS

Basically, vegetable purée soups are made with vegetables and the liquid in which they were cooked. Ingredients are reduced to a purée by pushing through a vegetable mill, rubbing through a sieve or blending in a liquidizer. The resulting purée is usually substantial enough to serve as it is and needs no thickening agent in the form of a roux or eggs or cream. Flavour and texture, however, can be improved if a little fat is used to sweat the vegetables before the liquid is added and to enrich them just before serving.

The vegetables

It is important to use fresh vegetables but because the vegetables are reduced to a pulp, purée soups offer an excellent and economic opportunity to use slightly overripe vegetables or foods which might otherwise go to waste, such as the outer leaves of lettuce, slightly tough end-of-season peas, watercress stalks or mushroom peel. You can make delicious soups using either a single vegetable or a judicious mixture of several vegetables.

Tubers such as potatoes and Jerusalem artichokes, root vegetables such as carrots, parsnips and turnips, cauliflower and pulses (dried peas, beans and lentils) will all purée to a thick soup after cooking.

Vegetables such as mushrooms, tomatoes, onions, celery, cucumbers, asparagus, spinach, lettuce and watercress do not have much substance in themselves. If used alone, very large quantities would be needed to create the right consistency for a purée soup. An additional vegetable (such as a potato) therefore is usually added to give the starchy ingredient which is necessary for thickening.

The liquid

Stock is probably the most frequently used liquid. Chicken or other white stocks are the most suitable because brown stocks can be too strong and might overpower the flavour of the vegetable. By all means use vegetable stock where suitable. For example, for pea soup make stock from the pea pods (see the chapter on stocks). The liquid from canned peas also makes excellent stock.

Vegetable cooking water may be used as a liquid base. Taste it first to check that the flavour is not overpowering as this could ruin a delicate soup. The water in which a cauliflower has been cooked, for instance, makes a valuable addition to parsnip soup.

Milk can be used, either on its own or with other liquids, but take care not to dilute it too much as this can cause curdling.

THE BASIC METHOD

Preparing the vegetables for a purée soup should be quick and easy. Clean all vegetables and, if necessary, peel them. There is no need to spend a lot of time peeling vegetables that are to be sieved because the skins will be caught in the bowl of the sieve. Roughly slice or chop the vegetables; it doesn't matter how small you chop them up as any goodness that escapes during cooking is captured in the soup. Using small pieces of food speeds up cooking time and saves fuel costs.

Sweating

Once you have prepared the vegetables, the next and very important step when making a hot vegetable purée soup is to sweat the vegetables as this will make them really tender and tasty.

To sweat vegetables, melt a little butter – about 25 g [1 oz] to 450 g [1 lb] vegetables – in a heavy-based saucepan. Oil can be used if preferred; vegetable or sunflower oil are best – olive oil would probably give too distinctive a flavour. Dripping, especially bacon dripping, can be used to advantage when you are making, say, a pea soup because the flavours are complementary. Margarine can be substituted for butter but it has nothing like the good, rich flavour of butter. Add the vegetables to the melted fat and shake the pan or stir to coat the vegetables all over. Cover and cook gently over low heat for 5-10 minutes to soften the vegetables and allow them to absorb the fat without burning.

Never be tempted to try to speed up this process by increasing the heat. Fast cooking would fry the vegetables and give them a hard outer skin which would stop the fat from being absorbed. Frying would also spoil the colour of the soup.

Plain and chilled soup: fat tends to coagulate when cold, spoiling texture and appearance, so sweating is always omitted when the soup is to be served chilled. The process is usually omitted, too, when a very plain and easily digested soup is being prepared as the fat would make it too rich. In these cases the prepared vegetables are cooked directly with the liquid.

Adding the liquid

After the vegetables have sweated for about 5 to 10 minutes and have absorbed most of the fat, pour on the cold liquid. Season lightly with salt and pepper and complementary herbs and spices, if used. Bring to simmering point, cover and simmer until ingredients are quite tender – about 15-25 minutes, depending on the vegetables used. Do not overcook, especially if you are using green vegetables or the flavour and colour will be lost.

Making the purée

There are three methods of puréeing the soups: using a vegetable mill, a sieve or a liquidizer. These pieces of equipment vary in price and in the final texture they achieve. However, they are all equally efficient so choose the machine to suit your needs and your pocket.

A vegetable mill is probably the most versatile method of puréeing because the resulting texture can be matched to suit the chosen ingredients by using the fine, medium or coarse attachment. A celery soup, for example, would require the fine grid to make it really smooth whereas the turnip and cucumber soup would be better if given a slightly coarser texture by milling the vegetables through the coarse grid.

Using a liquidizer is probably the quickest and easiest way of reducing the vegetables with their cooking liquid to a purée (although it may be necessary to sieve the soup after blending to remove fibres). A liquid-

Step-by-step vegetable purée soup

1 Melt butter in a pan. Add prepared vegetables, cover and sweat gently over low heat for 5-10 minutes.

2 After sweating, season and add liquid. Cover the pan and simmer for 15-25 minutes until tender.

3 To purée vegetables using a vegetable mill, hold over another saucepan and turn the handle.

4 To purée vegetables using a sieve, pour contents of pan into sieve, and press vegetables through.

5 To purée vegetables using a liquidizer, pour contents of pan into the goblet and blend.

6 Reheat soup gently over low heat. Adjust seasoning and enrich if desired. Do not allow to boil.

izer produces a consistently smooth result but in some cases this will be rather too textureless for a purée soup.

Serving

If the soup is to be served hot, reheat gently after puréeing and adjust seasoning to taste. Add more liquid if the consistency is too thick. If too thin, the soup can be simmered, uncovered, to reduce the quantity by evaporation – but this process is not effective when much thickening is needed. Enrich if you wish.

Enriching

This is an optional extra, done just before serving, to add a creamy texture and improve flavour. Simply stir small pats of butter, a little cream or sour cream into the soup. If the soup is to be served hot, stir over a low heat until warmed through but on no account allow it to boil or it may curdle, particularly if thin cream is used. For a more dramatic effect, dish the soup into individual bowls or a soup tureen and then add the cream by dribbling swirls over the top of the soup.

Serving cold soups

If the soup is to be served cold remember that the consistency can afford to be slightly thinner because soup thickens on cooling. The seasoning should be rather stronger since flavours appear to diminish when ingredients are chilled. Cool the soup, cover and chill thoroughly for about 3 hours before serving. Don't be tempted to speed up the chilling process by floating ice cubes in the soup – it will only dilute the flavours and make a watery soup.

STORING

Purée soups can be kept both in the refrigerator and freezer.

In the refrigerator: allow soup to cool and pour into a container with an airtight lid. Covered, the soup will keep for up to 4 days.

In the freezer: allow soup to cool. Pour soup into ice-cube trays. Freeze if necessary then empty cubes into plastic bags, seal and store in freezer. Alternatively, pour soup into an airtight container, leaving 12 mm [½"] head-space, and cover with the lid and freeze. Either way, the soup should keep for up to 2 months.

COMBINATION SOUPS

One vegetable alone makes a delicious soup, but a mixture of two or more vegetables can also be excellent and the addition of herbs and spices can improve both types. Here are a few ideas.

● Make a colourful soup from celeriac and tomatoes. Sieve the soup to remove tomato seeds and flavour with chopped chives and a little grated orange zest.

● Combine parsnip and apple and flavour with a little sage.

● Make a creamy soup from onion and cauliflower, and add a touch of colour by flavouring and garnishing with paprika or ground nutmeg.

● Fresh sorrel leaves make a delicious, strongly flavoured soup. Adding a little potato thickens the soup and will make it go further; stir in a generous amount of thin cream before serving.

● For potage bonne femme, a classic and economic French soup, use a mixture of leeks, carrots and potatoes, with a pinch of sugar to bring out the sweetness of the carrots.

● For a delicately flavoured and coloured courgette purée soup, do not peel the courgettes. Cook them in light chicken stock and flavour with chervil or dillweed.

● For Irish potato soup, simmer equal quantities of potatoes and onions in milk.

● For an instant iced tomato soup to rival gazpacho, crush a small garlic clove with salt. Put into a liquidizer with canned tomatoes and their liquid. Add a pinch of sugar, salt and pepper and a good squeeze of lemon juice. Sieve after liquidizing to eliminate tomato seeds.

Amounts to use for single vegetable purée soups		
Vegetable	**Liquid**	**Butter**
Carrots 450 g [1 lb]	550 ml [1 pt]	25 g [1 oz]
Celery 450 g [1 lb]	1.15 L [2 pt]	25 g [1 oz]
Courgettes 225 g [½ lb]	550 ml [1 pt]	40 g [1½ oz]
Leeks 450 g [1 lb]	550 ml [1 pt]	25 g [1 oz]
Mushrooms 225 g [½ lb]	550 ml [1 pt] half stock and half milk	25 g [1 oz]
Onions 450 g [1 lb]	550 ml [1 pt]	40 g [1½ oz]
Peas 700 g [1½ lb]	550 ml [1 pt]	25 g [1 oz]
Potatoes 450 g [1 lb]	550 ml [1 pt]	40 g [1½ oz]
Spinach 450 g [1 lb]	550 ml [1 pt]	25 g [1 oz]
Tomatoes 450 g [1 lb]	550 ml [1 pt]	25 g [1 oz]
Watercress (4 bunches) 450 g [1 lb]	1.15 L [2 pt]	

FRUIT PUREE SOUPS

Fruit purée soups are Scandinavian in origin and are very popular in those countries. Although it may sound strange at first to some tastes, in fact fruit purée soups have a deliciously delicate flavour and make a superbly refreshing beginning and, sometimes, end to a meal. Similar in method and resulting texture to vegetable purée soups, fruit purée soups are made from fresh, and sometimes from dried, fruit.

Fruit

For best results use fresh, ripe fruit. Apples, pears, cherries, apricots, plums, pumpkins, peaches, blackberries, raspberries, loganberries, strawberries and melons can all be used.

Of the dried fruit, apricots and prunes give best results; apples and pears can also be used.

Making fruit soup rarely involves sweating the fruit because the soup is always served cold and the fat tends to rise to the top and spoil it, and most fruit don't need the extra softening.

The liquid

Water, red or white wine, or a mixture of water and wine are the most commonly used liquids. Apple juice can be used in place of the white wine. Chicken stock or beef stock are sometimes used, usually with apple or pumpkin.

Thickening fruit soups

Fruit soups made with a single fruit which has a high water content (for example, cherries, plums and apricots) are thickened with cornflour. This is done after the fruit has been cooked. For every 450 g [1 lb] fruit and 1.15 L [2 pt] liquid you will need 30 ml [2 tablespoons] cornflour.

Flavouring

If you are serving the soup as a first course it may be flavoured with nutmeg, cinnamon, cloves, lemon peel or ginger and occasionally curry powder. Stir in fresh or sour cream or yoghurt just before serving.

If you are serving the soup as a pudding, stir in sweetened whipped cream and dust with nutmeg or cinnamon just before serving.

PREPARING THE FRUIT

Prepare the fruit by cleaning, peeling, coring, seeding or stoning until only fruit pulp is left. If you are puréeing the cooked fruit through a sieve or a vegetable mill, you can leave the skins and stones of apricots and plums intact as they will add extra flavour to the liquid and be strained off during puréeing.

Soak dried fruit overnight in the liquid to be used in the recipe.

Cooking the fruit

Put fruit in the saucepan and add the liquid and complementary flavourings. When both wine and water are used in the recipe, only the water is added at this stage. Wine is added after the fruit is puréed so that it is not simmered for a long time.

Bring to simmering point and simmer, covered, until ingredients are quite tender – about 10-25 minutes, depending on fruit used.

Making the purée

With the exception of berry fruit, purée in the same way as for vegetables using a liquidizer or vegetable mill. Only very fleshy berry fruit, such as strawberries, can be puréed in a vegetable mill. Smaller berry fruit such as blackberries, raspberries and loganberries are almost fleshless so purée these by sieving or by liquidizing and then sieving.

Before reducing the fruit to a purée spoon off and reserve some of the liquid if you want to thicken the soup.

Thickening the soup

In a medium-sized mixing bowl, blend 30 ml [2 tablespoons] cornflour into the reserved hot fruit juice. Stir the rest of the liquid into the cornflour mixture, then pour into the fruit purée. Add the wine, if used, at this stage. Bring to the boil over moderate heat, stirring, and simmer for 5 minutes.

Serving

Taste and adjust the seasoning. Enrich, as already described, if you wish. Serve cold in the same way as for vegetable purée soups.

TURNIP AND CUCUMBER SOUP

This soup makes excellent and economical use of the part of a vegetable which is usually discarded. It is served cold, so the vegetables are not sweated.

SERVES 4
225 g [½ lb] turnip tops
550 ml [1 pt] chicken stock
salt and pepper
1 medium-sized cucumber
250 ml [½ pt] sour cream
10 ml [2 teaspoons] freshly chopped dillweed

1 Wash turnip tops. Put into a saucepan, season and pour on the stock.

2 Bring to simmering point, cover and simmer for 20 minutes.

3 Reduce to a purée using a vegetable mill, sieve or liquidizer.

4 Peel and thinly slice cucumber. Stir into purée.

5 Allow to cool and then chill.

6 To serve, stir in sour cream and sprinkle with dillweed.

CREME DUBARRY

Although it is made of modest ingredients this is a luxury soup named after the mistress of the French king, Louis XV.

SERVES 4-6
65 g [2½ oz] butter
1 small cauliflower
1 celery stalk
1 medium-sized onion
salt and pepper
550 ml [1 pt] chicken stock
250 ml [½ pt] milk
pinch of ground nutmeg

1 Break cauliflower into florets. Slice onion and celery.

2 Melt 50 g [2 oz] butter in the saucepan and sweat vegetables in butter for 10 minutes, shaking pan occasionally.

3 Season and pour on stock and milk. Bring to simmering point, cover and simmer for 30 minutes or until vegetables are quite tender.

4 Reduce contents of pan to purée using vegetable mill, sieve or liquidizer.

5 Return soup to saucepan. Add nutmeg and reheat gently. Enrich the soup by stirring in the remaining butter cut into dice.

From Scandinavia, a deliciously cool fruit soup made from Morello cherries and white wine and flavoured with cinnamon.

CHILLED CHERRY SOUP

The recipe gives the stoned weight of cherries, so you will need to buy about 1 kg [2 lb] altogether. Morello cherries add good colour and flavour to the soup which should be served as a refreshing dessert. A cheap, dry white wine is adequate to cook in the soup. Just before serving garnish each bowl with 15 ml [1 tablespoon] thin cream, small macaroons and a few whole cherries.

SERVES 4-6
**450 g [1 lb] Morello cherries,
  stoned weight
225 g [½ lb] granulated sugar
half a cinnamon stick
1 lemon
30 ml [2 tablespoons] cornflour
400 ml [¾ pt] white wine**

1 Remove stalks and stone the cherries.

2 Place cherries in a medium-sized saucepan with the sugar, 550 ml [1 pt] water and the cinnamon.

3 Pare the zest from the lemon and add this to the pan.

4 Bring to simmering point, cover and simmer for 20 minutes.

5 Mix cornflour to a smooth paste with a little of the wine.

6 Stir the rest of the wine into the cornflour mixture and then pour into the soup.

7 Cook slowly, stirring until the soup comes to the boil and thickens slightly. Simmer for 5 minutes.

8 Remove and discard cinnamon and lemon rind.

9 Reduce contents of the pan to a purée using vegetable mill or liquidizer.

10 Allow to cool and then chill.

Variations
For chilled soups to start or finish a meal, use only 30 ml [2 tablespoons] sugar and replace the Morello cherries with any of the following flavours:

●450 ml [1 lb] pears. Replace the cinnamon with 5 ml [1 teaspoon] ginger.

●Combine cherries with pears and replace white wine with red.

●Make a plum or apricot soup from 450 g [1 lb] plums or apricots and 50 g [2 oz] sugar. Replace the white wine with water and garnish with sour cream.

●Try a combination of melon and strawberry. Garnish with whole, small strawberries.

POTAGE CRECY

This is one of the most economical purée soups, both in terms of time and cost of ingredients. Old carrots will give the best flavour, especially if cooked with a pinch of sugar to bring out their sweetness.

SERVES 4
450 g [1 lb] carrots
1 large onion, weighing about
   225 g [½ lb]
40 g [1½ oz] butter
salt and pepper
550 ml [1 pt] stock
5 ml [1 teaspoon] freshly
   chopped thyme

1 Clean and thinly slice carrots. Finely chop onion.

2 Melt the butter in the saucepan and sweat vegetables in butter for 10 minutes, shaking the pan occasionally.

3 Season and pour on stock. Add chopped thyme. Bring to simmering point, cover and simmer for 20 minutes or until vegetables are quite tender.

4 Reduce contents of pan to a purée using a vegetable mill, sieve or liquidizer.

5 Return soup to the saucepan. Reheat gently. Enrich with a pat of butter, if liked.

PEA SOUP

Weigh the peas after shelling. Ham stock gives a good flavour to the soup. Halve the quantity of peas if you are using dried peas.

SERVES 4
700 g [1½ lb] peas
4 spring onions
25 g [1 oz] butter
salt and pepper
1.15 L [2 pt] stock
10 ml [2 teaspoons] freshly
   chopped mint

1 Chop the onions. Melt the butter in the saucepan, sweat peas and onions in butter for 10 minutes, shaking the pan occasionally.

2 Season and pour on stock. Bring to simmering point, cover and simmer for 20 minutes or until vegetables are quite tender.

3 Reduce contents of pan to a purée using a vegetable mill, sieve or liquidizer.

4 Return soup to pan. Stir in mint and reheat.

Variations
●Use drained, canned peas and only 550 ml [1 pt] liquid, including some of the liquid from the can for additional flavour.
●Substitute fresh broad beans for the peas.

CURRIED APPLE SOUP

This recipe includes onion which would normally be softened by sweating in butter but because the soup is served chilled this is not done. Choose a crisp type of apple such as Cox or Granny Smith. To garnish the soup reserve some paper-thin slices of unpeeled apple brushed with a little lemon juice.

SERVES 6
700 g [1½ lb] dessert apples
1 small onion
2.5 ml [½ teaspoon] lemon juice
2.5 ml [½ teaspoon] turmeric
2.5 ml [½ teaspoon] ground
   cumin
2.5 ml [½ teaspoon] ground
   coriander
pinch of chilli powder
salt
a pinch of ground cloves
850 ml [1½ pt] chicken stock
150 ml [¼ pt] thin cream
90 ml [6 tablespoons] natural
   yoghurt

1 Peel, core and chop the apples. Peel and finely chop the onion.

2 Put apples and onion in a saucepan, cover with half the stock and seasoning. Cover the pan and simmer for about 10 minutes or until tender.

3 Reduce contents of pan to a purée using vegetable mill, sieve or liquidizer. Stir in the remaining stock.

4 Allow to cool. When cold, stir in the cream and yoghurt, cover and chill.

5 Just before serving stir in 150 ml [¼ pt] cold water if the soup seems too thick. Check for seasoning and add more salt and pepper if necessary.

6 Garnish with reserved apple slices.

GAZPACHO

This is a classic Spanish iced soup in which the vegetables are puréed raw. A liquidizer is best for the job – a sieve is totally unsuitable because of the raw, hard vegetables. Pass around small bowls each containing extra ingredients of cold croûtons, chopped olives, chopped cucumber, chopped onions and sliced hard-boiled eggs for each diner to sprinkle on top of his soup. This makes an excellent choice for a dinner party because it can be prepared well in advance but, as it is substantial, only serve small quantities of it.

SERVES 4
250 ml [½ pt] canned tomato
   juice
2 garlic cloves
half a cucumber
1 green pepper
1 red pepper
1 large onion
700 g [1½ lb] tomatoes
75 ml [3 fl oz] olive oil

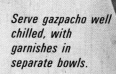

Serve gazpacho well chilled, with garnishes in separate bowls.

**30 ml [2 tablespoons] red wine
  vinegar
salt
freshly ground black pepper
half a sprig of marjoram
half a sprig of basil**

1 Peel and chop the cucumber. Remove white pith and seeds from green and red peppers and chop the flesh. Peel and chop the onion.

2 Blanch, peel, de-seed and chop the tomatoes. Chop the herbs. Peel and crush the garlic with a little salt.

3 Reduce all the ingredients to a purée using a liquidizer.

4 Add tomato juice. Increase quantity if the purée is very thick.

5 Chill for several hours in a refrigerator.

6 Stir well before serving.

Variation
If you don't have a liquidizer and are using a vegetable mill, reserve the tomato juice, oil, vinegar, salt and pepper while you purée the vegetables. Then stir in reserved ingredients.

JERUSALEM ARTICHOKE AND TOMATO SOUP
The subtle smoky taste of artichoke is ideal for a purée soup, but the colour is rather dull on its own so tomatoes are added to cheer it up. As you peel and slice the artichokes, keep a bowl of acidulated water near by to drop the artichokes into to prevent them from discolouring. Garnish the soup with crumbled grilled bacon or croûtons or, for a special occasion, with some fresh, pink prawns.

SERVES 4
**700 g [1½ lb] Jerusalem
  artichokes
1 large onion, weighing about
  225 g [½ lb]
25 g [1 oz] butter
225 g [½ lb] tomatoes
salt and pepper
1 garlic clove
850 ml [1½ pt] chicken or white
  stock**

1 Peel and thinly slice Jerusalem artichokes. Chop the onion.

2 Melt the butter in a heavy-based saucepan over low heat. Add the onion and artichokes. Cover the pan and sweat, shaking the pan occasionally, for about 5 minutes.

3 Meanwhile, skin the tomatoes, halve and remove seeds.

4 Add tomato flesh to the pan, cover and sweat for a further 3 minutes.

Fennel vichyssoise is a rich summertime soup.

5 Crush garlic and add to pan with salt and pepper. Pour on stock.

6 Bring to simmering point, cover and simmer for 15 minutes.

7 Reduce contents of pan to a purée using a vegetable mill, sieve or liquidizer.

WALNUT SOUP

This soup is particularly delicious when made with 'wet' walnuts – the very early season walnuts where the skins slip off easily and the nuts are slightly moist. If using fresh walnuts, dip them in boiling water and then slip off the skins. Buy 450 g [1 lb] to allow for the weight of the shells. The garlic flavour is not overpowering, but is an essential part of the soup.

SERVES 6
175 g [6 oz] walnuts, shelled weight
1 garlic clove
1.15 L [2 pt] chicken stock
150 ml [¼ pt] thick cream
salt and pepper

1 Peel and crush garlic clove with a round-bladed knife or garlic crusher.

2 Put walnuts and garlic in a saucepan, cover with stock and season. Cover the pan and simmer for about 15 minutes or until tender.

3 Reduce contents of pan to a purée using a vegetable mill, sieve or liquidizer.

4 Return soup to the saucepan. Add cream and reheat gently. Check seasoning.

CHILLED MELON SOUP

This soup should definitely take its place at the beginning of a meal. The cool, fruity flavour is sharpened by the addition of lemon juice and mint. The soup requires no cooking but must be well chilled before serving.

SERVES 6-8
2 large ripe honeydew melons
4 lemons
45 ml [1½ tablespoons] freshly chopped mint
pinch of ground cinnamon
125 ml [4 fl oz] natural yoghurt
150 ml [¼ pt] thin cream
sprigs of mint to garnish

1 Cut the melons in half. Discard the seeds and scoop out flesh.

2 Reduce melon flesh to a purée using vegetable mill, sieve or liquidizer.

3 Squeeze the lemons and add the juice to the purée.

4 Stir in the chopped mint and cinnamon.

5 Cover and chill.

6 Just before serving, beat the yoghurt and cream together until smooth, then stir into the soup.

7 Garnish with sprigs of mint.

FENNEL VICHYSSOISE

The distinctive flavour of Florentine fennel makes an unusual and delicious iced soup to serve on a warm evening. If you plan to liquidize the soup be sure to discard all the outer, tough, stringy pieces from the fennel bulb before cooking or it will not purée satisfactorily.

SERVES 4
350 g [¾ lb] Florentine fennel
550 ml [1 pt] water or chicken stock
salt and pepper
250 ml [½ pt] thick cream

1 Clean the fennel bulbs, discarding tough stringy pieces. Reserve ferny fronds for garnish. Chop the fennel.

2 Put the fennel in a saucepan, cover with water or stock and then season. Cover the pan and simmer for about 15 minutes or until tender.

3 Reduce contents of the pan to a purée using vegetable mill, sieve or liquidizer.

4 Allow to cool. When cold, stir in cream, cover and chill.

5 Garnish with reserved fennel fronds.

Soups

cream soups

Velvety smooth cream soups have a stunningly superior taste. Usually made from fresh ingredients, combined with a delicately flavoured béchamel sauce and enriched with cream and flavoured with a hint of herbs, they have a magical elegance about them that belies their modest cost and simplicity of preparation.

Cream soups are really one step up from the simple purée soup. They take longer to make than the purée soup, but you will find that the mouth-wateringly good results are worth the extra effort. Velouté soups, which are more complicated to make, are really very special and probably the classiest of all soups. However, cream soups are not really everyday fare—they are for occasions when you want to pull out all the stops to impress your guests, and they provide a contrast in flavour, texture and colour to following courses.

Cream soups are, as their name suggests, rich and creamy. The cream both binds the ingredients together to produce a particularly smooth consistency and makes the soup taste very rich. Also butter is stirred into hot cream soups just

before serving for glossy good looks.

Cream soups can be made from fish, poultry or vegetables. Red meat and fruit are never used. Usually the ingredients are cooked very gently in butter until tender (called sweating), then stirred into a thin béchamel sauce and reduced to a purée.

If root vegetables are used, thickening with béchamel is unnecessary. The starch content of the vegetable is a sufficient thickening so the ingredients are simmered in milk or stock and made into a purée. In all cases the soup is enriched with a final addition of cream or cream and butter just before serving.

Swirls of cream add to the eye appeal of this pale green lettuce soup, which can be served hot or cold.

THE INGREDIENTS
Vegetables

The vegetables that you use should be fresh but, as with purée soups, you can make good use of vegetable trimmings such as green leek tops or the outer leaves of a lettuce—even pea and bean pods make very good soups.

Almost any vegetable can be used to make a cream soup, apart from aubergine which is spongy in texture and doesn't give a good flavour. An unusual addition to the list is the stinging nettle which makes an excellent and really economical soup. Before you go out picking, equip yourself with thick gloves and a pair of kitchen scissors to cut through the rather woody stalk base. Once the nettles are cooked there is, of course, no sting left!

Nettles and all the green leaf family, including spinach, watercress and lettuce are suitable. Green beans, peas, tomatoes, mushrooms and leeks, as well as all root vegetables, such as Jersalem artichokes, make very good cream soups.

Very often a combination of two vegetables is used, one with a high starch content such as potato.

Poultry

The pale coloured flesh of chicken and turkey are ideal for making a cream soup. Any darker meat, such as beef or lamb, would ruin the colour of the soup and would also produce too strong a flavour. For the best results use the white meat from chicken or turkey, and discard the skin which does not have a particularly good flavour and does not purée well. The meat you use must always be cooked—and this provides an excellent way of using left-over chicken and turkey from a previous meal.

Fish and shellfish

The cooked flesh of cod or other white fish such as plaice, flounder, haddock, coley or whiting may form the basis of a fish cream soup. Be sure to remove all bones and skin before adding to the béchamel sauce. Of the shellfish, shrimps and prawns (which are supplied ready cooked) can be used to make a beautifully coloured cream soup. Carefully remove and reserve the shells before using—the shells may be used in a fish stock later.

The liquid

The liquid, either for the béchamel sauce or for cooking the vegetables themselves, may be milk, stock or water. Generally, milk is used for the green leafy vegetables so that the flavour of the vegetable is not overpoweringly strong and the colour is suitably delicate. Chicken or white stock is used for chicken cream soup and for other vegetables where its flavour will not overpower that of the main ingredient. A light vegetable stock may be used in the same way. Water may be used for tomato- and potato-based soups. Fish stock is used for fish soups.

Enriching

The extra rich flavour and smooth consistency of cream soups come from the final addition of cream and, in the case of hot soups, butter as well. The cream should be fresh and thick—thin cream would not give the same results. Measure the cream into a small bowl. Spoon in about 60 ml [4 tablespoons] of the hot soup and stir vigorously to mix thoroughly. The final addition of a little butter gives the soup an extra gloss.

EQUIPMENT

You will need the same equipment as described in the last chapter for puréeing. A vegetable mill with a fine grid is really better than a liquidizer for most soups with woody stringy matter that needs removing. Celery, for example, if liquidized needs sieving afterwards to remove any stringy matter.

You will also need a small bowl for mixing the cream, and a balloon whisk or spiral sauce whisk and sieve. A whisk is ideal for blending the creamy mixture from the bowl into the pan of hot soup and will do the job better than a wooden spoon. If lumps do occur when the creamy mixture has been added, a sieve can be used for straining. Conical sieves are specially shaped to speed up the process of straining liquids but an ordinary sieve could also be used.

BASIC METHOD
Using un-starchy vegetables

To make a cream soup with green leaf vegetables, or other un-starchy vegetables, such as tomatoes, make a béchamel sauce (see chapter on white roux sauces).

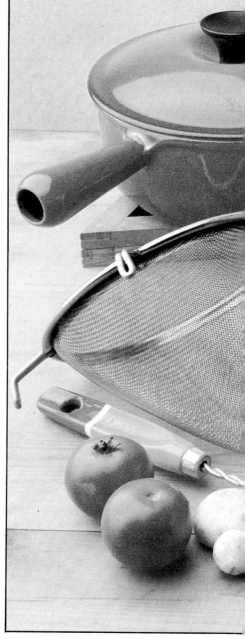

A heavy-based pan is needed for sweating vegetables. Purée soups with a liquidizer or vegetable mill. Whisk in cream with a beater. Strain with a conical strainer.

Always make a béchamel sauce and not a white sauce—the better quality of the béchamel is really worth the effort for these marvellous soups. The special flavour of the sauce is important in a cream soup which includes small quantities of vegetables.

Make the béchamel by infusing 550 ml [1 pt] milk with the flavourings. Then make a roux with 25 g [1 oz] each of butter and flour, add the strained milk, cover and simmer for 10 minutes. This gives a sauce of pouring consistency.

another vegetable, are made in the same way as for purée soups. Clean, peel and chop the vegetables and sweat them in a little butter for 5-10 minutes. Add stock or water according to the recipe and simmer until the vegetables are soft.

Reduce the contents of the pan to a purée using a vegetable mill, sieve or liquidizer. Reheat gently, season, thin and enrich.

Using chicken or turkey

A good cream soup can be made from chicken or turkey flesh. Cooked meat should always be used—preferably the white-coloured meat. Make a béchamel sauce from 550 ml [1 pt] well-flavoured chicken or turkey stock for every 175-225 g [6-8 oz] flesh. This is the weight required when the chicken or turkey is boned and skinned. Roughly chop the chicken or turkey meat (discarding the skin) and add this to the béchamel sauce. Simmer over gentle heat for 5 minutes to infuse the flavours. Reduce the contents of the pan to a purée using a vegetable mill or liquidizer—it is best to use a liquidizer here for really smooth results. A sieve would be impractical because of the difficulty of pushing the meat through, but the fine grid on a vegetable mill works satisfactorily. Reheat gently, season, thin and enrich as described overleaf.

Using fish and shellfish

For a cream soup using white fish such as cod, you will need 450 g [1 lb] white fish (including bones) to every 550 ml [1 pt] fish stock, which is made into a béchamel sauce.

Use fish which has been cooked by poaching, grilling or even boiled in the bag. Remove all the bones from the flesh with a fork.

If you are making a cream of shellfish soup you will need 225 g [½ lb] prawns or shrimps (in their shells) and 175 g [6 oz] cooked white fish.

Remove the prawns or shrimps from their shells and pound the flesh with a pestle in a mortar, or in a dish with the end of a rolling pin. Add this to the béchamel sauce. Simmer over gentle heat for 5 minutes to infuse the flavours. Reduce the contents of the pan to a purée using a vegetable mill or liquidizer. Sieving is impractical because of the bulk; it is best to use a liquidizer for puréeing fish soups. Reheat gently, season, thin and enrich as described overleaf.

Clean the vegetables and chop or slice them. Melt about 25 g [1 oz] butter in a thick heavy-based saucepan, add the vegetables, cover the pan and cook very gently for 5-10 minutes until most of the butter has been absorbed. This is called sweating. It is important to shake the saucepan or stir the ingredients occasionally to prevent them from burning and to ensure all the vegetables are evenly cooked.

Add the vegetables to the saucepan containing the béchamel sauce. Add complementary herbs, cover the pan and simmer gently over a low heat for 5-10 minutes to infuse the flavour of the vegetables and herbs in the sauce.

Reduce the contents of the pan to a purée using a vegetable mill, sieve or liquidizer, depending on ingredients used. If you are using a vegetable mill, it is best to use the finest grid to obtain a really smooth, well-blended soup.

Now check the soup for consistency. The final soup should be the consistency of thin cream so if it is too thick now, keeping in mind the final addition of cream will also thicken it slightly, thin the soup with a little stock or milk. Reheat gently, season, thin and enrich as described overleaf.

Using starchy vegetables

Cream soups that are made with a starchy vegetable such as potato, or with a combination of a starchy and

ADDING THE ENRICHMENT

A cream soup is enriched shortly before serving by the addition of thick cream, giving the soup its distinctive rich, smooth and creamy taste.

Place the thick cream in a mixing bowl and stir or whisk in about 60 ml [4 tablespoons] of the hot soup. Pour this blended mixture back into the soup in the saucepan. Stir or whisk the soup, using a spiral sauce whisk or balloon whisk, until blended. If you poured the cream directly into the hot soup, the cream could curdle and disperse in small globules across the surface of the soup.

Once the cream is smoothly incorporated, the soup should be reheated before serving. Stir the soup occasionally over a moderate heat, but do not on any account allow it to boil. If the soup were allowed to boil, the cream would be irretrievably spoilt.

Hot cream soups can be given an extra gloss by the final addition of butter. To do this, cut butter into small pieces—allowing 25 g [1 oz] butter per 550 ml [1 pt] soup. Stir butter pieces one by one into the hot soup just before serving. If you are serving the soup cold do not add butter because it would rise to the surface of the soup.

SERVING

Cream soups are served as the first course of a meal—since they are too rich to serve large enough portions for a main course. Use a cream soup to provide a contrast in flavour and colour to the courses following it— for example, a well-balanced meal would be cream of mushroom soup, grilled lamb and mixed salad followed by orange sorbet or a selection of cheeses. The meal would be dull and the effect on guests probably depressing if you served cream of leek soup, chicken with tarragon and cream followed by syllabub!

Have the soup as hot as possible, or really well chilled, before serving. Never serve the soup lukewarm. Because cream soups are so rich you will only need about 150 ml [¼ pt] of soup per serving.

Chilling: all vegetable cream soups may be chilled, but a chicken, turkey or fish soup should be served hot. To chill a vegetable cream soup, allow the soup to cool at room temperature for 30-40 minutes before covering and placing in the refrigerator for 3 hours.

Step-by-step cream soup

⧖⧖ *This method of making cream soups is suitable for unstarchy vegetables. The method is similar for poultry, fish and shellfish, where steps 4-6 are omitted. Make additions at step 7. For starchy vegetables, omit steps 1-3 and add liquid in step 7. To serve the soup chilled, omit the final addition of butter which would make the soup greasy.*

SERVES 4
1 large cucumber or 2 ridge cucumbers
1 medium-sized onion
salt
freshly ground black pepper
50 g [2 oz] butter
75 ml [3 fl oz] thick cream

For the béchamel sauce:
550 ml [1 pt] milk
half a small carrot
quarter of a celery stalk
1 bay leaf
salt and white pepper
pinch of nutmeg or mace
25 g [1 oz] butter
25 g [1 oz] flour

4 Meanwhile, wipe clean and chop the cucumber. Don't peel the cucumber as the skin will add colour. Peel and chop the onion.

5 Melt 25 g [1 oz] butter in a heavy-based saucepan over a gentle heat. As soon as the butter has melted add the vegetables.

9 Return the soup to the pan and place over a low heat. Taste and season lightly with salt and freshly ground black pepper.

10 Measure the cream into a small bowl. Spoon in about 60 ml [4 tablespoons] of the hot soup and stir vigorously to mix thoroughly.

1 Prepare vegetables and place them in milk with bay leaf. Bring slowly to the boil. Then cover and leave to cool for 30 minutes.

2 Make a roux with the butter and flour, remove from the heat and gradually stir in the strained re-warmed milk.

3 Return the pan to low heat and bring to the boil, stirring. Add salt, pepper, nutmeg or mace, cover and simmer for 10 minutes.

6 Cover pan and cook over gentle heat, shaking occasionally or stirring with a wooden spoon so vegetables cook evenly.

7 Add the softened vegetables to the béchamel sauce and simmer, covered, for 10 minutes to allow the flavours to infuse.

8 Reduce the contents of the pan to a purée using a vegetable mill, sieve or liquidizer. The liquidizer is probably the quickest to use.

11 Pour the cream and soup mixture back into the hot soup, whisking it in with a balloon or sauce whisk or stirring with a wooden spoon.

12 Reheat the soup carefully but do not allow it to boil or it will spoil. Meanwhile, cut the remaining butter into small pieces.

13 Stir or whisk the butter, one piece at a time, into the hot soup to give a final gloss. Adjust the seasoning and serve.

QUANTITIES FOR BECHAMEL-BASED CREAM SOUPS

Vegetable or meat	Béchamel sauce
artichoke, Jerusalem 350 g [¾lb] + 1 onion	550 ml [1 pt] milk based
asparagus 225 g [½ lb]	550 ml [1 pt] milk based
cauliflour 350 g [¾ lb] + 1 onion	550 ml [1 pt] milk based
celeriac 225 g [½ lb] + 1 onion	550 ml [1 pt] milk based
celery 450 g [1 lb]	550 ml [1 pt] milk based
chicken 175-225 g [6-8 oz] cooked meat	550 ml [1 pt] using chicken stock
chicory 225 g [½ lb]	550 ml [1 pt] milk based
cucumber 1 large or 2 ridge + 1 onion	550 ml [1 pt] milk based
fish 450 g [1 lb] white fish including bones	550 ml [1 pt] using fish stock
fish 175 g [6 oz] including bones + 225 g [½ lb] prawns including shells	550 ml [1 pt] using fish stock
leek 450 g [1 lb] + 1 onion and 1 carrot	550 ml [1 pt] milk based
lettuce 2 heads + 1 onion	550 ml [1 pt] milk based
mushroom 225 g [½ lb]	550 ml [1 pt] milk based
nettle 450 g [1 lb] + 1 onion	550 ml [1 pt] using white or vegetable stock
onion 450 g [1 lb]	550 ml [1 pt] using vegetable stock
pea 450 g [1 lb] shelled or frozen + 1 onion	550 ml [1 pt] using white stock
prawn or shrimp 225 g [½ lb] in shells + 1 onion and 1 carrot	550 ml [1 pt] using fish stock
tomato 450 g [1 lb] + 1 onion	550 ml [1 pt] using white or vegetable stock
turkey 175-225 g [6-8 oz] cooked meat	550 ml [1 pt] using chicken stock
turnip 450 g [1 lb]	550 ml [1 pt] milk based
watercress 225 g [½ lb] + 1 onion	550 ml [1 pt] milk based

Amounts of cream to use for enriching béchamel sauce based soups

275 ml [½ ml] soup—45 ml [3 tablespoons] cream
550 ml [1 pt] soup—75 ml [3 fl oz] cream
1.15 L [2 pt] soup—150 ml [½pt] cream
1.7 L [3 pt] soup—250 ml [½ pt] cream

For vegetables soups based on stock, milk or water
instead of béchamel, use double the quantity of cream.

Beautiful garnishes to float on well-chilled soup.

GARNISHES AND ACCOMPANIMENTS

The pale colour and smooth texture of cream soups lend themselves to crisp textures and strong colours of garnishes and accompaniments Decorate just before serving with julienne strips (matchstick-thin strips of vegetables such as raw carrot, celery, green or red peppers), paper-thin slices of cucumber or button mushrooms, chopped chives, sprigs of watercress, thinly sliced lemon, or extravagant swirls of thick cream. Alternatively, serve croûtons or crumbled crispy bacon or a few split almonds fried in butter until golden brown (particularly good with green bean soups). Whole peeled prawns add colour to fish soups, and chicken soup can be garnished with slivers of poultry breast. Serve garnishes (except for prawns and chicken slivers) in separate bowls so that guests may help themselves. In this way the garnishes remain crisp—floated in the soup too soon they would lose their texture and become soggy and unappetizing and may even sink.

STORING

The basic soup may be kept in a covered container in the refrigerator for a day or two but the cream should not be added until it is reheated for serving or the cream could go off. Any soup containing a large pro-

Choose appropriate decorations for each recipe.

portion of old potatoes may turn sour if kept any longer than this.

Freezing

Most soups freeze well although it is necessary to make some adjustments to the basic recipes. When making cream soups which are based on béchamel sauce for freezing, replace the flour in the sauce with cornflour. This is because soup which is thickened with ordinary flour tends to curdle on reheating. Don't freeze soups which have a large amount of potatoes in them because potatoes become slushy when frozen in a liquid.

If a soup recipe includes herbs and spices it is best to leave these out until the soup is defrosted for use. Cream is omitted because it is always added just before serving.

No soup should be kept in the freezer for longer than 2 months because it will develop a sour taste after this time.

Reheating

Allow the soup to defrost in the refrigerator or at room temperature. When liquid, place in a double saucepan and reheat it over gentle heat, stirring well. These precautions will stop the soup from separating. You may find that the soup has thickened with freezing and needs a little more stock or milk added to it on reheating. Adjust the seasoning, add the cream as described and serve.

CREAM OF LETTUCE SOUP

Instead of using 2 whole lettuces you could use the outer leaves of several lettuces and reserve hearts for salads. It is also a good way to use up lettuces which have gone rather too limp for a salad.

Serve hot or cold, depending on the weather. If serving cold do not enrich with butter. If serving hot accompany with croûtons.

The béchamel sauce is made with chicken stock to heighten the very delicate flavour of the lettuce.

SERVES 4
2 lettuces
1 small onion
salt
freshly ground black pepper
75 ml [3 fl oz] thick cream
50 g [2 oz] butter

For the béchamel sauce:
550 ml [1 pt] chicken stock
salt and white pepper
25 g [1 oz] butter
25 g [1 oz] flour

1 Make a roux with the butter and flour. Warm stock and stir in away from heat.

2 Return the pan to low heat and bring to the boil, stirring. Season with salt and pepper. Cover and simmer for 10 minutes.

3 Meanwhile, wash and dry the lettuces, peel and finely chop the onion.

4 Melt 25 g [1 oz] of the butter in the saucepan and sweat the onion and lettuce for about 10 minutes or until soft.

5 Add the onion and lettuce to the béchamel sauce and simmer, covered, for 10 minutes.

6 Reduce the contents of the pan to a purée using a vegetable mill, liquidizer or by passing through a sieve.

7 Return the soup to the pan, taste and season lightly with salt and freshly ground black pepper.

8 Measure the cream into a small bowl. Spoon in some of the hot soup and stir vigorously to mix thoroughly.

9 Pour the cream and soup mixture back into the hot soup, stirring all the time.

10 Reheat carefully but do not allow to boil. Meanwhile, cut the remaining butter into 5 or 6 pieces.

11 Stir the butter, one piece at a time, into the hot soup to give a final gloss. Adjust the seasoning and serve.

CREAM OF SPINACH SOUP

If you are using small young spinach leaves simply wash and cook them, stalks and all. Thick tough stalks of older spinach should be discarded. There is no need to chop the leaves but choose a pan large enough initially to fit them all in—they will soon decrease in size when cooked.

SERVES 4
450 g [1 lb] spinach
50 g [2 oz] butter
salt
freshly ground black pepper
75 ml [3 fl oz] thick cream

For the béchamel sauce:
550 ml [1 pt] milk
half a small carrot
quarter of a celery stalk
1 bay leaf
salt and white pepper
pinch of nutmeg or mace
25 g [1 oz] butter
25 g [1 oz] flour

1 Clean and chop the carrot and celery. Place them in the milk with the bay leaf. Bring slowly to the boil. Remove from heat, cover and leave to infuse for 30 minutes.

2 Make a roux with the butter and flour, remove from the heat and stir in the strained re-warmed milk.

3 Return the pan to low heat and bring to the boil, stirring. Season with salt, pepper and nutmeg or mace. Cover and simmer for 10 minutes'

4 Meanwhile, wash the spinach very thoroughly in a sinkful of cold, salted water. Drain, shake dry and discard any tough stalks.

5 Melt 25 g [1 oz] of the butter in a large saucepan over low heat.

6 Add the spinach, cover and sweat
for about 10 minutes or until soft.
Shake the pan or stir frequently so
that the spinach cooks evenly and
absorbs the butter without burning.

7 Add the spinach to the béchamel
sauce and simmer, covered, for 10
minutes.

8 Reduce the contents of the pan to
a purée using a vegetable mill,
sieve or liquidizer.

9 Return the soup to the pan, taste
and season lightly with salt and
black pepper. Reheat gently.

10 Measure the cream into a small
bowl. Spoon in some of the hot
soup and stir vigorously to mix
thoroughly.

11 Pour the cream and soup mixture
back into the hot soup, stirring all
the time.

12 Reheat carefully but do not allow
to boil. Meanwhile, cut the remaining butter into 5 or 6 pieces.

13 Stir the butter, one piece at a time,
into the hot soup to give a final
gloss. Adjust the seasoning and
serve.

Variations
●This soup can be made with frozen
spinach. Use 275 g [10 oz] frozen
spinach.
●For cream of mushroom soup,
replace the spinach with 225 g [½ lb]
mushrooms. Wipe clean and chop
them, reserving a few slices for
garnish. Use a vegetable mill for best
results.
●For sorrel and spinach soup,
replace half the fresh spinach with
sorrell leaves. An all-sorrel soup
would be to strongly flavoured.

*Hot spinach soup is made even more
delicious by scattering over crisp
croûtons just before eating.*

Add colour to cream of fish soup by garnishing with fresh prawns.

CREAM OF FISH SOUP

⊠⊠ *Any cooked white fish can be used in this extra fishy version; coley might replace the cod and thus offset the cost of buying the prawns. It is a marvellous way of using up left-over cooked fish, which has very few other uses, and yet the garnish of whole prawns makes the soup a luxuriously rich party dish. A crushed garlic clove adds good flavour to the soup which should be made with a good home-made fish stock.*

SERVES 4
450 g [1 lb] cooked cod
175 g [6 oz] prawns
1 garlic clove
salt and white pepper
75 ml [3 fl oz] thick cream
50 g [2 oz] butter

For the béchamel sauce:
550 ml [1 pt] fish stock
salt and white pepper
25 g [1 oz] butter
25 g [1 oz] flour

1 Make a roux with the butter and flour. Heat the stock and stir in away from the heat.

2 Return the pan to low heat and bring to the boil, stirring. Crush the garlic clove and add to the sauce with salt and pepper. Cover the pan and simmer for 10 minutes. Remove from the heat.

3 Meanwhile, remove skin and bones from the cod. Flake the flesh with a fork. Remove the shells from the prawns and pound in a mortar with a pestle, reserving a few whole prawns for the garnish.

4 Add the fish and prawns to the béchamel sauce and simmer, covered, for 10 minutes.

5 Reduce the contents of the pan to a purée using a vegetable mill or liquidizer.

6 Return the soup to the pan, taste and season lightly with salt and black pepper. Reheat gently.

7 Measure the cream into a small bowl. Spoon in some of the hot soup and stir vigorously to mix.

8 Pour the cream and soup mixture back into the hot soup, stirring all the time.

9 Reheat carefully but do not allow to boil. Meanwhile, cut the remaining butter into 5 or 6 pieces.

10 Stir the butter, one piece at a time, into the hot soup to give a final gloss. Adjust the seasoning and serve.

CREAM OF CHICKEN SOUP

This soup should be made with a well-flavoured chicken stock. The addition of lemon juice sharpens the soup to prevent it from tasting bland. Reserve a little of the chicken flesh, cut it into strips and garnish the soup with the strips just before serving.

SERVES 4
225 g [½ lb] cooked, skinned and boned chicken meat
5 ml [1 teaspoon] lemon juice
salt
freshly ground black pepper
pinch of nutmeg
75 ml [3 fl oz] thick cream
50 g [2 oz] butter

For the béchamel sauce:
550 ml [1 pt] chicken stock
salt and white pepper
25 g [1 oz] butter
25 g [1 oz] flour

1 Make a roux with the butter and flour. Warm the stock and stir in away from the heat.

2 Return the pan to low heat and bring to the boil, stirring. Season with salt and pepper. Cover and simmer for 10 minutes.

3 Meanwhile, chop the chicken meat into small pieces.

4 Add the chicken meat and lemon juice to the béchamel sauce and simmer, covered, for 10 minutes.

5 Reduce the contents of the pan to a purée using a vegetable mill or liquidizer.

6 Return the soup to the pan, taste and season lightly with salt, black pepper and nutmeg. Reheat.

7 Measure the cream into a small bowl. Spoon in some of the hot soup and stir vigorously to mix thoroughly.

8 Pour the cream and soup mixture back into the hot soup, stirring all the time.

9 Reheat carefully but do not allow to boil. Meanwhile, cut the butter into 5 or 6 pieces.

10 Stir the butter, one piece at a time, into the hot soup to give a final gloss. Adjust the seasoning and serve.

Variation
● A cream of turkey soup can be made with 225 g [½ lb] cooked turkey meat and 550 ml [1 pt] turkey or chicken stock.

VICHYSSOISE

This is an excellent example of how humble ingredients such as potato, onion and leeks can be turned into a spectacularly good soup. It is traditionally served chilled and tastes far better this way. Because of the addition of the starchy potato, this soup does not include a béchamel sauce.

SERVES 6
225 g [½ lb] potatoes
1 large leek
2 large onions
850 ml [1½ pt] chicken stock
salt
freshly ground black pepper
250 ml [½ pt] cream
25 g [1 oz] butter

For the garnish:
1 small bunch of chives

1 Peel and chop potatoes and onions. Wash the leek, remove most of the green part and discard. Chop.

2 Melt the butter in the saucepan and sweat the potato, onion and leek for about 10 minutes or until soft.

3 Pour over the stock and simmer, covered, for 25 minutes or until the vegetables are tender.

4 Reduce the contents of the pan to a purée using a vegetable mill, sieve or liquidizer.

5 Taste and season lightly with salt and freshly ground black pepper. Allow the soup to cool, then stir in the cream.

6 Chill the soup for about 3 hours. Just before serving, chop the chives and sprinkle over the soup.

Variation
● A really nourishing soup can be made of watercress (which contains vitamin A, vitamin C and iron) and potato. Wash one large bunch of watercress, remove tough stalks and chop. Reserve a few leaves for garnish. Peel and dice 450 g [1 lb] potatoes. Continue as for vichyssoise from step 2 and garnish with reserved watercress sprigs.
Velvety vichyssoise: many people think this the best of all chilled soups.

Sauces

white roux-based and sweet sauces

Smooth and subtly flavoured sauces are a cook's best friend. By following a few basic rules you hold the key to a whole repertoire of sauces which will add colour and variety to your meals, open up new avenues of cooking and quickly earn for you a reputation as an accomplished cook.

A simple, creamy well-flavoured sauce has countless uses in the kitchen. Everyday dishes such as

A smooth and creamy parsley sauce complements grilled fish

boiled or steamed cod, that sometimes look dull and unappetizing, can be turned into an eye-appealing dish by the simple addition of, say, a colourful parsley sauce—and every cook knows that good presentation of a dish means she is half-way to earning compliments and clean plates from all the family.

Savoury sauces can be used to complement a wide range of dishes—not only fish, but meat, poultry, egg, vegetable and pasta dishes. It may be part of the dish as in macaroni cheese, used to coat cooked foods such as chicken, or served in a sauceboat as an accompaniment.

A sauce not only complements a dish but it also increases the food value of a meal by adding milk, eggs, cheese and other nutritious ingredients. It may also form the basis of other dishes—croquettes, for instance, are bound together by a thick white sauce (panada) and, by the simple addition of whisked egg whites, you have a soufflé.

Last but not least, sauces are really an economy. They can make a dish go further, and they are invaluable for reheating cold foods that might otherwise languish in the larder and eventually go to waste.

The vast number of different sauces in use in the kitchen come from a few basic methods. When you have mastered these, the variations follow quite simply and logically. For this reason these basic sauces are often called 'sauces mères' (mother sauces).

A roux-based sauce is one made by blending flour into melted fat and then adding a liquid. There are three main types of roux-based sauces: white, velouté and brown. The first of these is discussed in this course.

Starch may also be used to thicken sauces which don't contain any fat. Arrowroot or cornflour are blended to a paste with a little of the liquid to be used and then cooked in the same way as a roux-based sauce. This is not strictly a white sauce because when the liquid is fruit juice it clarifies with cooking to make a clear sauce.

Both white and cornflour-based sauces can be used for sweet and savoury dishes. However, a white roux-based sauce is more commonly used for savoury sauces.

Cornflour and more especially arrowroot are very suitable for thickening fruit sauces because they clarify when cooked, leaving a clear fruity colour. However, cornflour can be used for savoury dishes when a more 'gluey' consistency is required: an example is the Chinese sweet-and-sour sauce.

WHITE ROUX-BASED SAUCES

The white roux-based sauce is probably the most versatile and commonly used of all the sauces. It is quick to make and marries well with meat, poultry, fish, eggs, and vegetables. The finished dish is often named after the sauce that is served with it, for example, sole mornay (sole with cheese sauce).

General principles

White and brown roux-based sauces are made in basically the same way. Butter, margarine or oil is melted in a saucepan and flour or cornflour, in equal quantities, is added to it and cooked until the butter has incorporated all the flour. The resulting paste is known as a roux.

A liquid, usually stock or milk or a mixture of the two, is added to the roux, and they are cooked together to form a sauce.

The proportion of fat and flour to the liquid depends on the consistency of the sauce required. In other words, whether it is to be used to coat food, to be poured from a sauce-boat or to bind food together (see chart of consistencies of roux-based sauces, overleaf).

Choosing ingredients

Fat: butter and margarine are both suitable for white sauce.
Flour: never use self-raising flour which has a raising agent added to it. Plain flour is nearly always used in preference to cornflour, which gives a slightly different texture and can make the sauce too gluey, especially when a thick sauce is required.
Liquid: the liquid is usually milk, or, if the sauce is to be served with chicken, fish, veal or some vegetables, it can be made with equal quantities of milk and a suitably flavoured stock.

Equipment

Stainless steel or heavy-based aluminium saucepans are best, because sauces tend to burn easily and may be spoiled in thin aluminium pans. However, this can be remedied if you invest in an asbestos mat which can be placed underneath a thin-based saucepan. This will reduce the heat and help prevent burning. All pans should have close-fitting lids to prevent evaporation of the liquid during cooking.

Ideally, you should have two saucepans—one for making small amounts and one for larger amounts of sauce. Choose a pan that will be three-quarters filled by the finished sauce. Too large a pan increases the area in which the sauce could burn underneath and over which it could evaporate.

Use a wooden spatula or spoon for stirring sauces because a metal one would scratch your pans.

You will find either a spiral sauce whisk or a balloon whisk useful, and, for correcting a lumpy sauce, you will need a nylon mesh or stainless metal sieve of about 15 cm [6"] in diameter to fit over the pan or, alternatively, use a liquidizer.

Techniques explained

Every potential sauce cook has a nagging fear of her sauce going lumpy and looking nothing like the velvety smooth version which is mocking her from the open pages of her cookery book! But it really is unnecessary to panic. By keeping some simple points in mind you should be able to sail through like a true professional.

Always ·weigh the ingredients before you start cooking. Sift the flour so that it is really fine, and never try to skimp on the proportion of butter to flour—you will only get a dull and lumpy sauce. Stick strictly to the quantities and ingredients given in the consistency and derivative charts shown on the following pages.

Melt the fat so gently over a low heat that it simply runs over the bottom· of the pan. Don't allow it to sizzle or it will quickly turn brown and ruin the delicate colour and flavour of the sauce. Draw the pan away from the heat when you add the flour and, later, the liquid, so that they can be worked in smoothly. After the flour has been added the pan is returned to the heat to allow the starch grains to burst and absorb the fat, giving a glossy finish to the finished sauce. Although professionals usually blend cold liquid into the hot roux, the beginner will find it easier to blend in a warm liquid. Heat the liquid until it is as hot as your finger can comfortably bear, take the roux off the heat, and pour in the liquid, a little at a time, stirring it constantly. This is done because it is easier to blend two foods together if they are approximately the same temperature.

Return the pan to the heat and bring to the boil stirring. Then reduce heat to very low, cover the pan and leave to simmer. Simmering enables the starch grains to expand and absorb the liquid thus thickening the sauce. Never be tempted to cut the cooking time (or the resulting sauce will have an unpleasantly overpowering floury taste), or to leave the sauce to boil—this would reduce the cooking time. It is important that the sauce just simmers, that is, when you can see a gentle agitation on the surface. Simmering temperature is from about 90° to 100°C [185° to 200°F].

It is worth remembering, too, that a little sauce goes a long way. Generally 250 ml [½ pt] of liquid will make a pouring sauce in a jug or cover portions for four people.

BECHAMEL SAUCE

◨ *This is not just a fancy French name*
◪ *for white sauce. The liquid is flavoured first, and it is always preferable to white sauce if you have the time to make it. The subtle flavour is especially good where there is either no further flavouring or where the additions are not dominant, for instance, hard-boiled eggs. Once the liquid has been infused with the flavourings, as shown here, the method is the same as for white sauce. Proportions given in this recipe make a coating sauce.*

MAKES 250 ML [½ PT]
half a small onion
half a small carrot
a quarter of a celery stalk
250 ml [½ pt] milk
bay leaf
25 g[1 oz] butter
25 g [1 oz] flour
salt and white pepper
pinch of nutmeg or mace

KEEPING AND REHEATING

If you need to make a roux-based sauce an hour or so in advance, the surface of the sauce should be covered with a dampened circle of greaseproof paper when still hot. This will prevent a skin forming.

Never reheat the sauce over direct heat: it may easily burn or become lumpy. Remove the paper and place the pan containing your sauce on a trivet in another larger pan so that the bottom of the saucepan is not in direct contact with the heat. Half fill the pan with water—a roasting tin is ideal—and place it over the heat. This improvised version of a bain-marie or

Step-by-step to white roux-based sauce

1 Melt the fat slowly in a small saucepan. Never let it sizzle or it will become brown and change the colour and taste of the sauce.

2 Remove pan from heat, stir in plain flour. Return to low heat, stir gently for 1-2 minutes until smooth. Do not let it colour.

3 Put liquid in a separate pan. Heat through until it is as hot as your finger can comfortably bear. On no account let it boil.

4 Remove the roux pan from the heat. Add a little liquid, stirring vigorously. Add the remaining liquid gradually, still stirring.

5 When the mixture is smoothly blended, return the pan to the heat and bring the sauce to the boil, stirring continuously. Season.

6 Turn the heat to low, cover the pan and simmer for 5 minutes to complete the cooking of the starch.

Step-by-step to béchamel sauce

1 Cut the vegetables into small squares (called dicing) and put into a pan with the milk and seasonings.

2 Slowly bring the milk to simmering point. Remove from the heat, cover and leave for 30 minutes for the flavours to infuse.

3 Strain the milk through a sieve into a jug. Discard the vegetables in the sieve. Continue from step 1 for a white roux-based sauce.

water bath will allow the sauce to be heated more gently, although it should still be stirred or beaten with a sauce whisk from time to time.

Storing
You may find it more convenient to make your basic roux in larger quantities and to store this in the refrigerator. When the roux is cold, turn it out of the saucepan into a screw-top jar. The roux will keep for a week in the refrigerator.

To use, weigh 50 g [2 oz] of roux for coating sauce (or 25 g [1 oz] for a pouring sauce or 100 g [¼ lb] for a panada). Put in a pan, heat 250 ml [½ pt] of liquid and proceed from step 4 for a white sauce, whisking all the time.

Freezing
To freeze a roux, allow it to cool, then put about 50 g [2 oz] on pieces of kitchen foil. When cold, wrap each piece in the foil. Put in polythene bags, seal and freeze for 3-5 months.

To use, drop the frozen or thawed roux into hot liquid and whisk in.

To freeze a made-up white sauce (add flavourings when reheating) pour the cooled sauce into waxed containers, seal, label and freeze. This will keep for 2-3 months. To use, thaw for 1-2 hours at room temperature and reheat in a bain-marie.

CONSISTENCY OF ROUX-BASED SAUCES

Consistency	Flour and butter	Liquid	Uses
Pouring sauces Should be thick enough to glaze the back of a wooden spoon at boiling point.	15 g [½ oz] each	250 ml [½ pt]	Basis for soups and accompanying sauces.
Coating sauce Should be thick enough to coat the back of a wooden spoon.	25 g [1 oz] each	250 ml [½ pt]	For coating foods.
Panada sauce Should be very thick at boiling point.	50 g [2 oz] each	250 ml [½ pt]	Basis for soufflés and binding foods together, such as croquettes

Prawns, mushrooms, celery, cheese and other fresh ingredients add nourishment and flavour to white sauces.

DERIVATIVES OF THE BASIC WHITE & BECHAMEL SAUCES
After the basic sauce is made, stir in the additions away from the heat just before serving

Sauce	Additions	Method	Serve with
Anchovy 250 ml [½ pt] béchamel sauce	5 ml [1 teaspoon] anchovy essence		Poached or steamed fish.
Caper 250 ml [½ pt] béchamel sauce	15 ml [1 tablespoon] capers 15 ml [1 tablespoon] lemon juice	Liquid for béchamel equal quantities of milk and fish or white stock.	Boiled mutton, roast lamb or tripe. Boiled bacon.
Celery 250 ml [½ pt] béchamel sauce	2 celery stalks, 10 ml [2 teaspoons] lemon juice	Chop celery. Boil for 15 minutes. Purée.	Chicken or ham.
Cheese 250 ml [½ pt] white sauce	40-50 g [1½-2 oz] Cheddar cheese, 2.5 ml [½ teaspoon] dry English mustard	Finely grate the cheese. Stir cheese and mustard in just before serving.	Vegetables, pasta, egg or fish dishes.
Egg 250 ml [½ pt] béchamel sauce	1 egg	Hard boil the egg. Sieve yolk and chop white.	Steamed or poached white fish.
Mornay 250 ml [½ pt] béchamel sauce	50 g [2 oz] gruyère or Parmesan cheese 40 g [1½ oz] butter	Finely grate cheese.	Veal, chicken, eggs, vegetables and pasta.
Mushroom 250 ml [½ pt] béchamel sauce	50 g [2 oz] mushrooms 15 g [½ oz] butter	Thinly slice mushrooms. Sauté in butter. Liquid for béchamel: equal quantities of milk and chicken stock.	Roast or boiled chicken.
Mustard 250 ml [½ pt] white sauce	5 ml [1 teaspoon] English mustard, 5 ml [1 teaspoon] white wine vinegar, 5 ml [1 teaspoon] caster sugar	Liquid for sauce: equal quantities of milk and fish stock.	Fried or baked mackerel or herring.
Onion 250 ml [½ pt] white sauce	225 g [½ lb] onions, 25 g [1 oz] butter, 25 ml [1 fl oz] thin cream (optional)	Sauté onions until soft, but not brown. Purée with butter and cream.	Tripe, lamb or veal.
Parsley 250 ml [½ pt] béchamel sauce	15 ml [1 tablespoon] chopped parsley		Bacon, white fish or vegetables.
Prawn 250 mpl [½ pt] white sauce	75 g [3 oz] prawns or shrimps 10 ml [2 teaspoons] lemon juice 2.5 ml [½ teaspoon] anchovy essence, or 15 ml [1 tablespoon] tomato ketchup	Liquid for white sauce: equal quantities of milk and fish stock. Chop prawns or shrimps.	White fish
Tarragon 250 ml [½ pt] béchamel sauce	15 ml [1 tablespoon] freshly chopped tarragon		Chicken

CORRECTING MISTAKES

What went wrong	Cause	Remedy
Lumpy sauce	Fat too hot when flour was added; or roux not cooked sufficiently; or liquid added too quickly without stirring enough. Lumps in sweet sauce indicate insufficient mixing of the starch and liquid, or insufficient stirring.	Push the hot sauce through a nylon or wire sieve into a clean pan. Or blend in a liquidizer for 1-2 minutes at high speed. Reheat carefully, stirring vigorously.
Raw flavour or dull sauce	Insufficient cooking of the starch.	Continue cooking.
Thin sauce	Wrong proportions of ingredients, over-cooking or undercooking of the roux.	Thicken by reducing the liquid. Place the saucepan over high heat and boil rapidly until the consistency is right. Stir continuously to prevent burning.
Thick sauce	Wrong proportions used or sauce allowed to evaporate during cooking.	Gradually beat in more hot milk or stock. Test again for seasoning.
Greasy sauce	Too much fat or overcooking of the roux, which causes the fat and flour to separate.	Remove pan from heat and use paper towels to soak up the surface fat.

SWEET SAUCES

There are plenty of sweet sauces in tubs and packets and tins sold today, but none is as good or as cheap as those you can so easily make yourself. Now that cream is so expensive it is well worth learning to make some of those tangy fruit and creamy sauces which were once the natural accompaniment to baked and steamed puddings, stewed and poached fruit, hot soufflés and pancakes.

Although sweet sauces are made from a starch base and not the roux of the savoury sauces, the method of cooking is very similar and the same rules apply to cooking the starch.

Basic sweet pouring sauce

This is the simple starch-thickened sauce which can be made with milk, fruit juice or water with other flavourings blended with cornflour or arrowroot. It is not strictly a white sauce except when the liquid is milk, or cream is added.

Arrowroot is generally used to thicken a fruit sauce because it gives a completely clear sauce and has the advantage of needing only a short cooking time. Never boil an arrowroot sauce for longer than specified in the recipe because it will lose its thickening qualities and the sauce will quickly become thin again. Starch-thickened sweet sauces may be made in advance and reheated in the same way as the roux-based sauces.

Sweet sauces are usually served from a sauce-boat at the table, although they may be poured over ice-cream before serving. Allow 250 ml [½ pt] of sweet sauce for four servings.

Flavouring sweet sauces

Simple milk sauces can be flavoured with 5 ml [1 teaspoon] of mixed spice or nutmeg, or 30 ml [2 tablespoons] of jam or marmalade—excellent with steamed puddings. The grated rind of half an orange or lemon adds a tangy taste to sauces made with fruit juice or water. For special occasions, turn your sauce into something special by flavouring with 30 ml [2 tablespoons] of rum, sherry, brandy or almost any liqueur. A richer sauce can be made by stirring in 30 ml [2 tablespoons] of thin cream.

Step-by-step to basic sweet sauce

▽ This basic recipe can be adapted to
▲ make any number of delicious sweet sauces to serve with ice-cream or piping hot puddings. Granulated sugar is used as it dissolves easily and does not colour the sauce. This amount will feed four people generously.

MAKES 250 ML [½ PT]

250 ml [½ pt] milk, fruit juice or water
15g [½ oz] cornflour or 7 g [¼ oz] arrowroot
25 g [1 oz] granulated sugar flavouring
15 g [½ oz] butter, optional

1 In a medium-sized mixing bowl, mix the starch with 30 ml [2 tablespoons] of the cold liquid, stirring continuously until thoroughly blended.

2 In a medium-sized saucepan, dissolve the sugar in the remaining liquid over medium heat, stirring until dissolved. Bring to the boil.

Pears in a hot chocolate sauce make an impressive dessert. Surround the pears with scoops of ice-cream just before serving.

3 Remove pan from the heat and pour the hot liquid in a gradual stream into the starch mixture, stirring continuously until blended.

4 Return the sauce to the pan and boil over medium heat for 3 minutes for cornflour or 1 minute for arrowroot, stirring all the time.

5 Add the flavouring. Just before serving, whisk in the butter with a balloon or sauce whisk to give a glossy finish.

Handy hints

- Keep a vanilla pod in a container of sugar and use this flavoured sugar in recipes where vanilla is required.
- Place a vanilla pod in the milk or other liquid used in the recipe when this is heated. The vanilla pod may then be removed, dried and stored for re-use until its flavour is too weak.
- Use vanilla essence—2-3 drops of essence is enough for 250-550 ml [½-1 pt] liquid. Always choose a good quality essence and test its strength before use.

Variations

- For chocolate sauce, melt 50 g [2 oz] plain chocolate in the sugared milk, or mix 15 ml [1 tablespoon] cocoa powder with the liquid.
- For a less sweet chocolate sauce, add 2.5 ml [½ teaspoon] instant coffee powder with the cocoa and starch to the sugared milk.
- For a coffee sauce, blend 15 ml [1 tablespoon] instant coffee powder with the starch and add to the sugared milk. Or use 50 ml [¼ pt] each of strong coffee and milk, add sugar and flavour with 2-3 drops of vanilla essence, or use vanilla-flavoured milk or sugar (for details see handy hints).
- For ginger syrup sauce, make the basic sauce with all water, or half water and half syrup from a jar of preserved ginger. Dissolve 100 g [¼ lb] Demerara sugar in the water or syrup mix, and add a small piece of lemon peel and 2-3 drops of lemon juice. Leave for 10 minutes, then remove the peel. For special occasions, add one or two pieces of preserved ginger cut into small pieces at the end of cooking time.
- For a butterscotch sauce using water, dissolve 125 g [¼ lb] Demerara sugar in half the water. Add 25 g [1 oz] butter and thinly pared rind of half a lemon. Bring to the boil and simmer for 5 minutes. Strain through a sieve into a clean saucepan and discard the peel. Blend the arrowroot with the remaining water and continue as for basic recipe. Add juice of half a lemon just before serving.
- For orange sauce, omit the sugar use 250 ml [½ pt] made-up frozen (or canned) orange juice and flavour with 5 ml [1 teaspoon] grated lemon zest.
- For a tangy lemon sauce, use the juice of 1 lemon and make up the rest of the liquid with water. Flavour with 5 ml [1 teaspoon] grated lemon zest.

CHICKEN VOL-AU-VENTS

This is a very economical way of spreading left-over cooked chicken among a number of people. These light vol-au-vents make an excellent lunch dish for 4 people. As a first course they will serve 8 people.

SERVES 4-8
175 g [6 oz] cooked,
**   boned and skinned chicken**
50 g [2 oz] mushrooms
8 individual vol-au-vent cases

For the sauce:
250 ml [½ pt] milk
half a small onion
half a small carrot
a quarter of a celery stalk
bay leaf
salt and white pepper
pinch of nutmeg or mace
25 g [1 oz] butter
25 g [1 oz] flour
5 ml [1 teaspoon] lemon juice

1. Prepare the vegetables for the béchamel sauce and infuse them in the liquid.

2. Heat the oven to 200°C [400°F] gas mark 6. Shred the chicken and thinly slice the mushrooms.

3. Sauté the mushrooms in a little butter until soft.

4. Meanwhile, make a roux in a small saucepan. Remove from heat.

5. Add the infused milk to the roux and stir. Season, cover and let it simmer for 5 minutes.

6. Stir mushrooms and chicken into the sauce. Season with lemon juice, salt and pepper.

7. Remove the tops and spoon in enough mixture to fill each vol-au-vent case, pressing well into the case with the handle of a spoon. Put the tops back in place.

8. Place vol-au-vents on a baking tray and heat for about 15 minutes.

HAM AND LEEKS AU GRATIN

Chicory may be substituted for the leeks.

SERVES 4
8 medium-sized leeks
8 slices of ham
4 slices of wholemeal bread
50 g [2 oz] butter

For the sauce:
50 g [2 oz] butter
50 g [2 oz] flour
550 ml [1 pt] milk
salt and pepper
5 ml [1 teaspoon] dry English mustard
100 g [¼ lb] Cheddar cheese

1. Trim and wash the leeks. Steam them for 20 minutes until tender.

2. Meanwhile, make a roux in a small saucepan. Remove from the heat.

3. Heat the milk, add to the roux and stir. Season, return to heat and

bring to boil stirring. Cover and let it simmer for 5 minutes.

4 Grate the cheese and add, with the mustard, to the white sauce.

5 Wrap each leek in a slice of ham and place in an ovenproof dish. Pour over the sauce.

6 Make breadcrumbs and heat grill to medium.

7 Top the dish with the bread-crumbs, dot with butter and brown under medium heat.

Variations

●For a simple cauliflower cheese, boil or steam a whole cauliflower and keep hot until needed. Pour over. 550 ml [1 pt] cheese sauce, sprinkle over 100 g [¼ lb] grated Cheddar cheese and grill under medium heat.
●Boil or steam cauliflower florets. Add 100 g [¼ lb] sliced spiced sausage to 550 ml [1 pt] cheese sauce and pour over the cauliflower. Sp-

rinkle over grated cheese and brown under medium heat.
●Arrange slices of hard boiled eggs and tomatoes in a buttered gratin dish and pour over 550 ml [1 pt] cheese sauce. Sprinkle over grated cheese and cook in the oven at 200°C [400°F] gas mark 6 for 15-20 minutes. Sprinkle over crisply fried smoked bacon and garnish with sliced tom-atoes.
●Cook 225 g [½ lb] macaroni in plenty of boiling salted water for 8-10 minutes. Drain, mix with 550 ml [1 pt] cheese sauce and pour into dish. Top with 50 g [2 oz] grated cheese and brown under medium heat.
●For a more substantial dish, fold in 3 slices of chopped ham and 225 g [½ lb] skinned and chopped tomatoes to the macaroni mixture.

Serve creamy kedgeree or chicken vol-au-vents for a simple lunch or supper dish. Both are made with a delicately flavoured béchamel sauce which lightly binds the ingredients together.

CREAMY KEDGEREE

◸◹ *This is a creamy mixture of smoked fish, rice and an egg sauce. It is an ideal dish to prepare in advance. To reheat, cover with buttered greaseproof paper and place in a moderate oven for about 25 minutes.*

SERVES 4
450 g [1 lb] boil-in-the-bag smoked haddock fillets
275 g [10 oz] long-grain rice
salt and black pepper
pinch of cayenne pepper
15 ml [1 tablespoon] freshly chopped parsley

For the sauce:
250 ml [½ pt] milk
half an onion
half a carrot
a quarter of a celery stalk
bay leaf
pinch of nutmeg or mace
25 g [1 oz] butter
25 g [1 oz] flour
1 medium-sized egg

1 Prepare vegetables and infuse in the milk with the bay leaf and nutmeg. Cover and set aside.

2 Put the rice, salt and 700 ml (1¼ pt) cold water into a large saucepan. Bring to the boil and stir once.

3 Immediately reduce the heat as low as possible. Cover the pan and simmer for 15 minutes without removing the lid or stirring.

4 Meanwhile, cook haddock according to manufacturer's instructions, and make the sauce.

5 Melt the butter slowly in a pan. Stir in the flour away from the heat. Return to the heat and cook stirring for 1-2 minutes.

6 Add the milk to the roux away from the heat, a little at a time, stirring vigorously.

7 Return the pan to the heat, bring to the boil, stirring. Cover and simmer for 10 minutes.

8 Hard boil the egg.

9 Turn the haddock out of its bag into a bowl, remove and discard the skin and flake the fish.

10 Test the rice by biting a few grains. If not quite tender, or if the liquid is not completely absorbed, replace the lid and cook for a few minutes longer.

11 Arrest cooking of egg by plunging in cold water. Shell the egg, chop the white and sieve the yolk.

12 Add flaked haddock, rice, egg and seasonings to the béchamel sauce. Stir well over moderate heat for 3 minutes or until it is hot.

13 Remove the pan from the heat and pile the mixture on to a warmed serving dish. Garnish with parsley.

CHOCOLATE PEARS

Here is a delicious combination: dessert pears poached in a flavoured syrup, served with ice-cream and hot chocolate sauce. The pears can be prepared an hour or two in advance if wished. The addition of butter gives the sauce a glossy finish.

SERVES 4
4 ripe dessert pears
350 g [¾ lb] caster sugar
1 vanilla pod
4 cloves
ice-cream

For the chocolate sauce:
250 ml [½ pt] milk
50 g [2 oz] dark chocolate
15 g [½ oz] cornflour
25 g [1 oz] granulated sugar
15 g [½ oz] butter

1 Peel the pears, leaving the stalks on. Remove the 'eye' from the base and level off to stand upright.

2 Choose a pan which is large enough to stand all the pears in. Put the sugar in the pan and add 550 ml [1 pt] water.

3 Bring to the boil, stirring, and then boil for 2 minutes.

4 Remove syrup from heat. Add vanilla and cloves, then carefully stand the pears in the pan.

5 Cover the pan and poach over low heat for 15-20 minutes until the pears are tender. Spoon the syrup over the fruit occasionally during cooking.

6 Lift the fruit out of the pan with a perforated spoon and place in a serving dish. Cool, cover and chill in a refrigerator for 30 minutes.

7 Put the cornflour in a small bowl and stir in a little cold milk to make a smooth paste.

8 Put the rest of the milk in a saucepan, add the broken chocolate and sugar, and stir over a moderate heat until the chocolate has completely melted.

9 Pour the hot chocolate liquid into the cornflour mixture and stir in.

Rødgrød and chocolate cream are two economical ways of using the sweet sauce method to make chilled creamy desserts.

10 Return the liquid to the pan and bring back to the boil. Cook for 3 minutes over a low heat, stirring continuously.

11 Add the butter in small pieces and beat with a balloon whisk until glossy. Cover and keep on a low heat.

12 Remove the pear dish from the refrigerator and uncover.

13 Surround the pears with scoops of ice-cream and pour the sauce over the pears, or serve separately in a sauce-boat.

RODGROD

Puréed fruit is used to make this smooth Scandinavian dessert which slips down your throat. It only takes a short time to prepare, but you should allow 2 hours chilling time. The amount of sugar to use varies according to the ripeness of the fruit. Fresh redcurrants are often tart.

SERVES 6
1 kg [2 lb] fresh or canned redcurrants
1 kg [2 lb] fresh or frozen raspberries
45 ml [3 tablespoons] arrowroot
100 g [¼ lb] caster sugar
50 g [2 oz] shredded almonds
150 ml [¼ pt] whipped cream

1 Purée the fruit (see chapter on purée soups) and mix together. Drain canned fruit first.

2 Mix the arrowroot with 30 ml [2 tablespoons] of the cold purée. Put the rest of the purée in a saucepan and bring to the boil over low heat, stirring continuously.

3 Remove pan from heat and gradually pour the hot liquid into the starch mixture, stirring continuously until blended.

4 Return the sauce to the pan and boil over medium heat for 1 minute, stirring all the time.

5 Sweeten to taste and allow to cool.

6 Meanwhile, put the almonds in the base of the grill pan and place close under medium heat to brown for 2 minutes. Reserve.

7 Pour the purée mixture into individual serving glasses and chill.

8 Before serving, decorate with whipped cream and sprinkle with toasted almonds.

CHOCOLATE CREAM

A simple chocolate sauce can be transformed into a rich dessert by the addition of whipped cream. This is still an economical chocolate pudding to serve to a family since it is based on cocoa and milk, rather than on real chocolate and eggs, as with some rich party sweets. You can, however, present it like a party sweet. Serve it in individual custard glasses or cocottes. Decorate with one of the following: 50 g [2 oz] chopped hazelnuts, 20 ml [4 teaspoons] chocolate-coloured sugar strands, or place a single crystallized violet in the centre of each pudding.

SERVES 4
250 ml [½ pt] milk
15 g [½ oz] cornflour
15 ml [1 tablespoon] cocoa powder
3 ml [½ teaspoon] instant coffee powder
25 g [1 oz] granulated sugar
150 ml [½ pt] whipped cream

1 In a medium-sized mixing bowl, mix together starch, cocoa and coffee powder with 30 ml [2 tablespoons] of the cold milk, stirring continuously until thoroughly blended.

2 Put the remaining milk into a medium-sized saucepan. Add the sugar and stir over medium heat until it is dissolved. Then bring the liquid to the boil.

3 Remove pan from the heat and gradually pour the hot liquid on to the starch mixture, stirring continuously until blended.

4 Return the sauce to the pan and boil over medium heat for 3 minutes, stirring all the time.

5 Allow to cool completely.

6 When cold, fold in the whipped cream and pour the mixture into individual serving dishes.

7 Decorate before serving.

Sauces

velouté sauces

Velouté sauces are a traditional part of classical French cookery but, unlike some classical recipes, velouté sauces are amazingly quick to make—and the results are stunningly good. Made with basic ingredients such as home-made stock, fresh eggs and cream, velouté sauces take you a step up the ladder from béchamel sauces to a most impressive style of cookery.

Velouté, as the name implies, means velvety and this is an aptly named sauce. The velouté sauce is really the rich relation of the basic béchamel sauce—richer both in colour and texture. A slightly cooked roux and the use of a well-flavoured stock instead of the rather bland milk gives a richer biscuit colour, and the final addition of egg yolks and cream makes it richer in texture.

Like the basic béchamel sauce, the vélouté sauce is a sauce mère (mother sauce). Once you've mastered the technique of making it, you hold the key to many other classical French sauces, as you can see from the family tree chart.

Velouté sauces are perhaps the most useful of all the roux-based sauces; their creamy flavour and light texture can be used to coat poached chicken, veal, fish or plainly boiled or steamed vegetables. In fact, because the sauce is so rich, the food it complements should ideally be as simple as possible—the simpler the better. Velouté sauces also form the basis of a whole range of delicately flavoured soups, which are described in detail in a later course.

Velouté sauce, and sauces derived from it, is always made to a coating

consistency. Because it is so rich, a little goes a long way. A sauce made with 250 ml [½ pt] liquid and 25 g [1 oz] each of fat and flour is enough for 4 people when it accompanies a dish.

Small pieces of cooked chicken or turkey, poached in stock or left over heated in a velouté sauce, and this mixture can be used to make a complete dish (often called a blanquette), or to fill light puff pastry vol-au-vents, flan cases or pancakes to make mouth-watering starters, lunch or supper dishes.

Once you have mastered the simple white sauce, you will find that making velouté is simply a natural step up the ladder to a really impressive style of French cookery.

EQUIPMENT AND TIMING
To make a velouté sauce you will need the same equipment as that needed for the white roux-based sauces (see the previous chapter). You will also need a small measuring jug, a small mixing bowl, a fine sieve and a whisk. A conical sauce sieve is the best type of sieve to use as it is specifically designed to speed up the process of straining liquids. The use of a sauce whisk or balloon whisk gives a glossy look to the final sauce.

It takes less time to make a velouté sauce than to make a béchamel sauce. It should take you no more than 30 minutes including the preparation of flavourings.

INGREDIENTS
The ingredients used for a velouté sauce are similar to those for a béchamel or white sauce. It is important to use the very best ingredients—this is intended to be a really superb, classical sauce and it deserves all the attention and careful choice of ingredients to give the best results.

Fat
Choose either salted or unsalted butter for the fat. Butter gives the best flavour and colour to the sauce, and it is a pity to go to the trouble of making a velouté sauce and then economize on a few pence worth of fats. In emergencies margarine can be used instead of butter, but in this case do not attempt to colour the roux at all since this is almost impossible to do with margarine. Never use oil or

dripping—both would give the final sauce the wrong flavour, and oil will not colour.

Flour
Plain, sifted flour should be used except when you are making the sauce for freezing. In this case, use cornflour rather than flour and it will keep longer. Never use self-raising flour—your sauce does not need a raising agent.

Liquid
The liquid used for a velouté sauce should be a strong, well-flavoured stock. Chicken, veal or fish stock may be chosen according to the food with which the sauce is to be served. This stock may be taken from the pot in which the chicken or fish for the meal is cooking, or made separately.

Eggs and cream
The final addition of fresh thick cream and egg yolks gives all the velouté sauces their particular delicacy and richness. Cream and yolks are blended together (this is called a liaison) and added to the sauce towards the end of cooking time, thus thickening and binding the sauce. Use the yolks from medium-sized eggs and fresh thick cream. Don't try to economize by using thin cream because it will not give the same results.

BASIC METHOD
To make a basic velouté sauce, first prepare the mushrooms which are used to add taste—they are an optional extra, but they really do give the sauce a good flavour. Either whole mushrooms or mushroom trimmings can be used. Allow 3-4 small mushrooms (or the equivalent in peelings and stalks) to every 250 ml [½ pt] stock. Chop the mushrooms as finely as possible—the more cut surfaces there are the more the mushroom flavour will leak out into the sauce. Place the chopped mushrooms on one side.

Measure the stock that you will be using, pour it into a small, heavy-based saucepan and place over low heat to heat through gently.

Choose a small heavy-based pan in which to make the sauce. Put the butter into it and melt over low heat.

Remove the pan from the heat and stir in the flour to make a roux. You will need 25 g [1 oz] each of fat and

Step-by-step to velouté sauce

MAKES ABOUT 250 ML [½ PT]
25 g [1 oz] butter
25 g [1 oz] flour
250 ml [½ pt] hot chicken, veal or fish stock (depending on final dish)
3 or 4 small mushrooms or mushroom peelings or stalks finely chopped (optional)
1 egg yolk
30 ml [2 tablespoons] thick cream
salt
freshly ground black pepper
2-3 drops lemon juice

4 Add the chopped mushrooms or mushroom peelings and stalks if these are being used.

8 Add 75 ml [5 tablespoons] of the hot sauce to the liaison, a little at a time, stirring well.

1 Melt butter in a saucepan over gentle heat. Remove from heat and stir in the flour to make a roux.

2 Return pan to low heat and cook roux, stirring for about 4 minutes until it turns a pale fawn colour.

3 Quickly remove from heat. Gradually add hot stock, stirring to keep the mixture smooth.

5 Return to heat. Bring to boil stirring. Reduce heat, cover and simmer for 15 minutes.

6 Meanwhile place the egg yolk and cream in a small bowl and mix thoroughly with a fork or whisk.

7 Remove pan from heat and strain the sauce through a fine sieve into a clean heavy-based pan.

9 Pour the contents of the bowl into the pan in a steady stream, whisking or stirring as you do so.

10 Season to taste with salt and pepper and add 2-3 drops of lemon juice, but no more.

11 Return saucepan to low heat. Bring the sauce to boiling point, stirring continuously. Serve.

flour to every 250 ml [½ pt] stock.

Return the saucepan to low heat and cook the roux, stirring continuously, for about 4 minutes until it turns a very pale fawn colour. Watch carefully and take the pan away from the heat immediately the roux has changed colour. This point is very important because an essential characteristic of the sauce is the cooking of the roux to a straw or fawn colour (another name for velouté is fawn sauce). Never allow the roux to brown.

While the pan is away from the heat, add the hot stock, slowly at first, stirring all the time to incorporate it smoothly.

When all the hot stock has been stirred in, add the finely chopped mushrooms to the saucepan and return the pan to medium heat. Bring the sauce to the boil, stirring all the time.

Cover the pan, reduce to low heat and simmer the sauce for 15 minutes, stirring occasionally so that the full flavour of the mushrooms infuses with the sauce. Continue to stir the sauce from time to time.

While the sauce is simmering, place the egg yolk and cream in a small mixing bowl and blend them together with a fork or whisk to make the liaison. Allow 1 egg yolk and 30 ml [2 tablespoons] thick cream for every 250 ml [½ pt] of liquid used to make the sauce. Then remove the saucepan from the heat and strain the hot, well-flavoured sauce through a fine sieve into a clean heavy-based saucepan. This will remove the mushrooms and, conveniently, get rid of any lumps that might possibly have occurred! The mushrooms left in the sieve can be used for other dishes such as shepherds pie or a spaghetti sauce to provide bulk but will not, of course, give much flavour as most of this will have gone into the sauce.

Add egg yolk and cream liaison to the sauce. It is essential that this is done away from the heat. First add a few spoonfuls of the hot sauce to the liaison in the bowl and whisk or stir to mix thoroughly. Then pour the contents of the bowl in a steady stream into the hot sauce, beating all the time with a whisk or spoon until everything is incorporated. Never try to save time by adding the liaison directly to the hot sauce without the initial blending, because the sauce and liaison would not mix well and might curdle.

Lemon juice (2-3 drops for 250 ml [½ pt] sauce) is now added to the sauce to give it a subtle tangy taste. Do be frugal with the amount you use—if you add too much the flavour of the sauce will be overpowered by the acid taste and this cannot be rectified without spoiling the balance of ingredients.

Finally, return the pan to low heat and bring the sauce just to boiling point, stirring all the time, to allow the egg yolk to cook and thicken the sauce.

As soon as the sauce has reached boiling point remove the saucepan from the heat and use the sauce. Do not allow the sauce to continue boiling once boiling point has been reached.

SAUCES DERIVED FROM VELOUTE SAUCE

Basic velouté sauce is excellent in its own right, but like béchamel sauce it is a 'sauce mère' (mother sauce) and lends itself to a wide range of flavourings. Additional ingredients alter the flavour (but not the texture) of the basic velouté to produce 'daughter' sauces, many of which are as famous as velouté itself.

To make a sauce derived from velouté make the basic velouté as shown in the step-by-steps but omit the mushrooms in step 4 (because their flavour may conflict with the taste of the substitute ingredients). Unless otherwise specified, at step 10 add the extra ingredients specific to the particular sauce you are making. Always prepare the ingredients before you begin to make the sauce, so they are ready to use when you want them. All the derivative sauces given here are based on the use of 250 ml [½ pt] stock.

● For a velouté herb sauce, make a basic velouté sauce and flavour it with a few finely chopped sprigs of your favourite herb and pour over meat, fish or vegetables.

● For a rich garlic-flavoured sauce crush a garlic clove and add this with a bouquet garni and 4 whole peppercorns to the sauce. Strain the sauce just before serving and discard flavouring ingredients.

● For a velvety curry sauce, stir 5 ml [1 teaspoon] curry powder into the hot stock. This is added to the sauce early on as the curry spices need to be cooked for a while so that they develop properly.

● For a colourful paprika sauce stir 5 ml [1 teaspoon] ground paprika into the hot chicken stock.

● For a mushroom sauce, chop 50 g [2 oz] mushrooms. Place in a small saucepan, just cover with water and a squeeze of lemon juice. Bring to the boil, simmer for 1 minute, strain and pat dry. Add to a hot velouté sauce just before serving so that the colour of the sauce is not spoilt by dark mushroom juices. The flavour is improved when making this sauce if mushrooms are also used in step 4.

● For a Bercy sauce simmer 2 finely chopped shallots in 75 ml [3 fl oz] white wine in an uncovered pan until the wine is reduced by half. Stir wine and shallots into the velouté sauce, which has been made with fish stock, and just before serving stir in 25 g [1 oz] butter and 10 ml [2 teaspoons] finely chopped parsley.

● A spicy polonaise sauce can be made by stirring 76 ml [3 fl oz] sour cream or plain yoghurt, 5 ml [1 teaspoon] each of grated horseradish (or horseradish sauce), finely chopped fennel and lemon juice into a velouté sauce made with chicken stock. (The lemon juice used here is in addition to the basic velouté sauce lemon flavouring.)

● For poulette sauce make a basic velouté sauce with veal stock and stir in 10 ml [2 teaspoons] finely chopped parsley and 5 ml [1 teaspoon] lemon juice just before serving. Again, lemon juice is in addition to the basic velouté sauce lemon flavouring.

● For a suprême sauce, make a velouté sauce using strong chicken stock and replace the basic liaison with 3 egg yolks and 150 ml [¼ pt] thick cream.

● For a Chivry sauce boil together for 5 minutes a handful of spinach and 2-3 sprigs each of tarragon, chervil and chives. Drain and reduce to a purée by rubbing through a sieve.

This should give just under 15 ml [1 tablespoon] of purée. Stir this into the basic sauce made with chicken or fish stock so that it is coloured to a delicate green.

COOKING AHEAD
Ideally, a velouté sauce and any of the derivative sauces should be made just before serving, but you can make any of these sauces in advance and successfully store or freeze and reheat—providing you make the basic sauce only (up to step 5 in the step-by-step pictures). Liaisons and final flavourings must not be added until the sauce is reheated, just before serving.

Making in advance
If you make a velouté sauce an hour or two before it is needed, lay a circle of buttered greaseproof paper on the surface of the hot sauce to stop any skin forming. Set the sauce aside until it is required.

Storing
It is well worth making a larger quantity of basic velouté sauce than you need. Store some in the re-frigerator in a covered container for use on another day as the basis of a soup or a sauce. It will keep for three or four days in this way.

Freezing
If you wish to freeze a velouté sauce, make the basic sauce but use cornflour rather than flour for the roux. Made in this way the sauce will keep for up to two months. Allow the sauce to defrost in the refrigerator before reheating.

Reheating
To reheat the basic sauce it is best to use a double boiler or bain-marie to be sure that the bottom of the pan is not in direct contact with the heat and that no lumps will form. Place the sauce in the top of a double boiler, or place the pan containing your sauce on a trivet in a pan half-filled with water, and reheat slowly over a gentle heat, stirring until the mixture is hot. If the sauce is at all lumpy strain it through a fine sieve into a clean pan. When the mixture is hot and smooth, gradually add the egg and cream liaison as described in the basic method.

Bercy
Add: white wine, shallots, butter and parsley.
Uses: this is a famous sauce which is traditionally served with poached fillets of sole, but you could also use plaice. Pour the sauce over the hot fish in a gratin dish and place under a hot grill to glaze the surface—it will only take 2 minutes.

Polonaise
Add: sour cream or yoghurt, horse-radish, fennel and lemon juice.
Uses: a good spicy sauce to serve with grilled lamb cutlets and steaks. Serve in a sauce-boat.

Poulette
Add: freshly chop-ped parsley and lemon juice.
Uses: for coating chicken breasts or escalopes of veal, or pour over young broad beans, new potatoes or carrots before serving.

Suprême
Add: egg yolks and thick cream.
Uses: the ideal sauce to coat a suprême (breast) of chicken. Also excellent poured over hot sliced bacon or ham.

Garlic
Add: garlic, bouquet garni and black pep-percorns.
Uses: for coating egg, vegetable and poultry dishes.

These dishes show some of the ways in which velouté-based sauces can be used. From left to right: new potatoes and mushroom velouté; sole with Bercy sauce; slivers of chicken breast and curry sauce; and paprika sauce in a sauce-boat.

RICH FISH VOL-AU-VENT

This delicately flavoured fish dish based on a Bercy sauce can be served in one large or eight small vol-au-vent cases. It is an excellent way of using up left-over cooked fish. Any white fish such as cod, plaice or coley can be used. Butter is whisked into the sauce at the end of cooking time to add an extra gloss and a rich flavour.

SERVES 4
275 g [10 oz] cooked white fish
100 g [¼ lb] shelled prawns
1 large or 8 small, cooked vol-au-vent cases

For the Bercy sauce:
2 shallots
75 ml [3 fl oz] white wine
50 g [2 oz] butter
25 g [1 oz] flour
250 ml [½ pt] hot fish stock
a sprig of parsley
salt
freshly ground black pepper
1 egg yolk
75 ml [3 fl oz] thick cream
half a lemon

1 Put the vol-au-vent on a baking sheet and place in the oven at 160°C [325°F] gas mark 3 to heat through while preparing the filling.

2 Remove and discard all skin and bones from the cooked white fish. Flake the fish with a fork.

3 Roughly chop the prawns using a mezzaluna or sharp knife.

4 Peel and finely chop the shallots. Place in a small saucepan, pour on the wine and simmer, uncovered, until the wine is reduced by half.

5 Melt 25 g [1 oz] of the butter in another saucepan over low heat.

FROM VELOUTÉ

Chivry (simple)
Add: tarragon, chervil and chives.
Uses: for fish or chicken breasts, this sauce contains chopped herbs.

Chivry (traditional)
Add: spinach, tarragon, chervil and chives.
Uses: this delicately green-coloured sauce looks superb poured over simple white fish such as sole or plaice, or poached chicken breasts.

Curry
Add: curry powder.
Uses: coat poached eggs, chicken or turkey breasts on a bed of rice.

Paprika
Add: paprika.
Uses: a delightful, delicately coloured sauce to coat poached or soft-boiled eggs, cooked chicken or turkey breasts.

Mushroom
Add: button mushrooms.
Uses: for coating escalope of veal, chicken breasts or new potatoes.

Remove from the heat and stir in the flour to make a roux.

6 Return the pan to low heat and cook the roux, stirring, for about 4 minutes or until it turns a very pale fawn colour.

7 Remove the pan from the heat and add the hot stock gradually, stirring continuously to keep the mixture smooth.

8 Stir in the shallots and wine. Return the pan to the heat and bring to the boil, stirring continuously.

9 Cover the pan and simmer for 10 minutes, stirring occasionally.

10 Stir in the chopped prawns and flaked white fish and continue simmering for a further 5 minutes.

11 Place the egg yolk and cream in a bowl and mix thoroughly with a fork or whisk. Add about 75 ml [5 tablespoons] of the hot sauce to the liaison, a little at a time and stirring well.

12 Pour the contents of the bowl into the saucepan, pouring in a steady stream and whisking or stirring the sauce all the time. Season to taste

and add 2–3 drops of lemon juice.

13 Cut the remaining butter into little pieces. Finely chop the parsley.

14 Return the sauce to the heat. Bring to boiling point, whisk in the butter and finely chopped parsley and remove immediately from the heat.

15 Pour the mixture into the hot vol-au-vent cases, cover with pastry lids and serve.

Variation
● This rich fishy filling can be used to fill a 20 cm [8″] cooked pastry case, or 8 pancakes.

ONIONS IN POULETTE SAUCE

This quickly made vegetable dish is an excellent accompaniment to simple roasts, boiled or grilled meat dishes. Choose onions of equal size so that they will be cooked at the same time. The mushroom flavouring is omitted when making the sauce as the onions have a strong enough flavour themselves. The sauce chart gives suggestions for other vegetables that can be served in this way.

SERVES 4
450 g [1 lb] small onions

For the poulette sauce:
25 g [1 oz] butter
25 g [1 oz] flour
250 ml [½ pt] hot chicken stock
1 egg yolk
30 ml [2 tablespoons] thick cream
salt
freshly ground black pepper
2–3 parsley sprigs
half a lemon

1 Melt the butter in the saucepan over gentle heat. Remove from the heat and stir in the flour.

2 Return the pan to low heat and cook the roux, stirring for about 4 minutes until it turns a pale fawn colour.

Hungarian eggs are served on toast. Onions in poulette sauce should accompany simple meat dishes.

3 Remove from the heat and add the hot stock gradually, stirring continuously to keep the mixture smooth.

4 Return the pan to the heat, and bring to the boil, stirring continuously. Cover and simmer for 15 minutes, stirring occasionally.

5 Meanwhile, skin the onions but leave them whole. Place them in a saucepan of cold, salted water and bring to the boil. Cover and simmer for about 8 minutes or until just tender.

6 Wash and finely chop the parsley and squeeze the lemon.

7 Place the egg yolk and cream in a small bowl and mix thoroughly with a kitchen fork to make the liaison.

8 Remove the saucepan from the heat and add about 75 ml [5 tablespoons] of the sauce to the

liaison. Add it a little at a time, whisking or stirring well.

9 Pour the contents of the bowl into a saucepan. Pour it in a thin stream, stirring or whisking all the time.

10 Return the saucepan to the heat. Bring the sauce to boiling point and immediately remove the pan from the heat. Season.

11 Drain the onions, place in a warmed serving dish and pour over the sauce.

HUNGARIAN EGGS

This dish is quick to prepare and makes a nourishing start to a meal. The paprika flavouring is added with the stock when making the sauce to allow plenty of time for it to cook thoroughly and give its full flavour to the sauce. A base of crisp toast soaks up the egg yolk from the soft-boiled egg—you can use white or wholemeal bread.

SERVES 6
6 medium-sized eggs
6 slices bread
1 pimento, canned

For the paprika sauce:
25 g [1 oz] butter
25 g [1 oz] flour
250 ml [½ pt] hot chicken stock

5 ml [1 teaspoon] paprika
1 egg yolk
30 ml [2 tablespoons] thick cream

1 Cut the pimento lengthways into twelve thin strips.

2 Cut the bread into rounds with a large pastry cutter. Or place a large cup upside down on the bread and cut around the rim.

3 Toast the bread on both sides and keep warm.

4 Melt the butter in a small heavy-based saucepan over low heat.

5 Remove the pan from the heat and stir in the flour.

6 Return the pan to low heat and cook the roux for 4 minutes, until it is a pale fawn colour.

7 Remove the pan from the heat and stir in the hot stock, gradually at first, until it is thoroughly combined. Add the paprika.

8 Return the saucepan to low heat and bring to the boil, stirring.

9 Cover the pan, reduce heat and simmer for 15 minutes, stirring occasionally.

10 Meanwhile, soft boil the eggs. Arrest cooking by plunging them in cold water for 1 minute. Shell the eggs and put them in a bowl of warm water.

11 Place egg yolk and cream in a small bowl and blend together with a fork or whisk.

12 Remove the saucepan from the heat and add 75 ml [5 tablespoons] of the hot sauce to the egg and cream liaison.

13 Gradually pour the contents of the bowl into the saucepan, whisking or stirring all the time.

14 Return the saucepan to low heat and gradually bring to boiling point, stirring. As soon as the sauce reaches boiling point, remove the pan from the heat and cover.

15 Place the toast on warmed individual plates. Pat the eggs dry and place one on each piece of toast.

16 Carefully spoon some of the hot sauce over each egg.

17 Arrange 2 pimento strips in a cross over each egg and serve immediately.

Star recipe

BLANQUETTE DE VEAU

This delicious and classic party dish of tender veal and vegetables is lightly coated with a delicate and creamy velouté sauce flavoured with veal stock. Choose close-textured meat that is pale pink, soft and moist. Avoid flabby, wet meat. The meat is blanched (brought to the boil) and rinsed before cooking to remove the unattractive grey scum that initially rises to the surface of the pan. Serve garnished with triangles of fried bread. This provides a crisp contrast in textures. To add colour to the dish, these may be coated with chopped parsley. Hold the fried triangle by one corner and dip into melted butter and then into freshly chopped parsley, then arrange round the dish. Accompany the veal with hot fluffy rice or creamed potatoes and buttered green beans.

SERVES 6

1 kg [2–2½ lb] veal from the shoulder or knuckle, boned weight
1 medium-sized onion
24 baby onions
4 carrots
juice of half a lemon
1 bouquet garni
salt
freshly ground black pepper
100 g [¼ lb] butter
50 g [2 oz] flour
2 egg yolks
150 ml [¼ pt] thick cream
100 g [¼ lb] button mushrooms
5 ml [1 teaspoon] lemon juice

3 Place the veal in large pan three-quarters full of cold water. Bring to boil over medium heat.

4 Remove the saucepan from the heat and drain the veal into a colander.

5 Rinse the meat under cold running water. Drain and dry the meat on kitchen paper.

9 Return the meat and vegetables to the saucepan. Cover the pan and set aside.

10 In a pan, melt 50 g [2 oz] butter. Make roux away from heat. Stir over low heat until pale fawn.

11 Measure 850 ml [1½ pt] of reserved stock and stir into the roux away from the heat.

1 Peel carrots and onions. Chop carrots and finely chop medium onion. Leave baby onions whole.

2 Trim away and discard any veal fat. Cut meat into even-sized cubes, about 40 mm [1½″] square.

6 Rinse pan. Add meat, carrots, chopped onion, lemon juice, seasonings and bouquet garni.

7 Pour on just enough water to cover. Bring to boiling point, cover and simmer for 1½ hours.

8 Remove the saucepan from the heat and drain the liquid through a colander into a bowl. Reserve.

12 Bring to the boil, stirring, cover and simmer for 15 minutes. Meanwhile mix the liaison.

13 Away from the heat, stir a little sauce into the liaison. Whisk or stir liaison into saucepan.

14 Pour sauce into meat pan, cover and simmer for 10 minutes so meat absorbs sauce flavour.

15 Place the baby onions in a pan and just cover with cold water. Cover and simmer for 5–8 minutes.

16 Wipe mushroom caps clean with a damp cloth. Trim the stalks level with the caps.

17 Put the butter, mushrooms and lemon juice in a saucepan. Cover and simmer for 5 minutes.

Pile the hot veal on to a serving dish. Place the mushrooms and onions at each end and surround with fried bread triangles.

Sauces

brown sauces

A brown sauce, smoothly and carefully blended, enriched with herbs and simmered for a long time to develop its flavour, is the basis of many classic French dishes. The secrets of a successful brown sauce are in its seasoning and in the careful reduction of the liquid to achieve the right consistency and to concentrate the flavour.

Brown sauces are one of the glories of French cooking, and are exacting to make. There is, however, no mystery about them. The principles of their construction are the same as for white and velouté sauces covered in the previous two chapters.

Once you have mastered the basic techniques and practiced one or two of the classic sauces and gained confidence, the variety of sauces to be made is almost endless. The combinations and quantities can be varied according to what is available and your personal taste.

BASIC BROWN SAUCES
There are four basic brown sauces—simple brown sauce, jus lié, sauce espagnole and demi-glace.

Simple brown sauce: this is a modest household sauce suitable for everyday use. For this, a few vegetables are browned in fat, flour is added and cooked to form a brown roux, then brown stock is added and simmered. Good stock is desirable but the simple sauce is the only one of the four classic brown sauces that should be attempted with a bouillon cube or light vegetable stock in an emergency. This sauce takes about an hour to make.

Jus lié: the French name means juice with a binder or thickening agent. This is a much quicker alternative to simple brown sauce, taking about five minutes. Arrowroot or cornflour is used as an addition (liaison) to the basic stock and then cooked to thicken it. It is essential, therefore, to make this sauce with really good quality stock, because nothing is added in the way of vegetables or herbs and spices to give it extra flavour.

Sauce espagnole: this is a superior version of simple brown sauce. It is made by the same method, but is more time consuming and has more elaborate ingredients. Instead of a few simple vegetables as before, a variety of chopped vegetables is used. A flavoured fat such as bacon is included. The combination of the vegetables and the bacon is called a mirepoix in French. Flour is added and cooked to make a brown roux as with a simple brown sauce. The stock and herbs are added and cooked as before, but there are further additions in the form of tomatoes and further simmering takes place. The whole sauce takes about two hours to make.

Demi-glace: this is the 'crème de la crème' of brown sauces—its French name means a half-glazed sauce as it has a slightly shiny appearance. For this you should make an espagnole sauce (this need not be on the same day), then add more brown stock. This addition must be of the best quality brown stock (called a fond brun) made of meat bones. The sauce is then simmered again until reduced and refined to a half-glaze. (Half-glaze is the name given to sauces which are so reduced and refined that they will set to jelly when cold.) This sauce could take two and a half hours to make.

USES OF BROWN SAUCES

All the four basic sauces outlined above can be served with a variety of dishes. Indeed espagnole and demi-glace will make any dish special. However, they can also be used as the basis for a new creation, where additions are used to change and subtly enhance them. Espagnole and demi-glace are usually used for the richest and most luxurious sauces.

Jus lié and the simple brown sauce are the cheapest and quickest to make, which makes them the fastest practical way of lifting your daily cooking to a more accomplished level.

Espagnole is always preferable to the simple brown sauce and well worth making if time permits, and always worth preparing for a special occasion.

Demi-glace is for purists, people with plenty of time, for those odd occasions when fond brun (best quality brown stock) is plentifully available, and for when you are really trying to impress.

Dishes with brown sauces

Brown sauces are associated in most people's minds with meat and game, and it is true that they may be shown to best advantage when served in this way. There are many famous dishes which are named after the sauce which adorns them, for example clams à la diable, duck bigarade and tournedos chasseur. Recipes for many of the classic dishes follow in later courses.

However there are many more modest dishes, made from chicken, pork and veal with brown sauces, and even eggs are good served in this way. Vegetables, particularly if they have been cooked by boiling or steaming and then drained, are delicious served with one of the brown sauces. The sauce makes the vegetable into a subtle vegetarian meal with no hint of parsimony, rather the reverse!

These sauces may also be used as binders in dishes such as chicken and ham pie, or with fillings for vol-au-vents, or to bind rechauffés (reheated meat and vegetables).

EQUIPMENT

The equipment used for making brown sauces is the same as that needed for the white roux-based group. You must, however, take care not to leave the wooden spoon in the roux, because this reaches a high temperature and there is a risk that the spoon could burn.

A sieve is essential for finishing a brown sauce. One with a strong nylon mesh is best, particularly when wine or vinegar is being used, as a metal sieve could taint the flavour. It must be big enough to fit over a saucepan or bowl. The conical sauce sieve (called a chinois strainer) which fits inside the basin is traditional for the job. Its big advantage is that the sloping sides help the liquid to drip through quickly.

A double boiler or bain-marie is needed for reheating the made sauce. If you do not have one you can improvise with a pan or bowl on a trivet inside a larger pan containing boiling water.

INGREDIENTS

The ingredients and the method for three of the sauces brunes (brown sauces) are similar to those used for the white roux-based sauce given in

an earlier chapter. The fourth jus lié, is not a roux-based sauce at all, but is made in the same way as the sauces made with a starch liaison in that course.

Differences between brown and white roux

Like the white-roux sauce, the three principle brown sauces are based on a combination of fat and flour which is cooked; a liquid is then added and cooked to form a thickened sauce. Simple brown sauce, sauce espagnole and demi-glace, like white sauce and velouté, are all sauces mères (foundation sauces of French cookery).

The first difference between white and brown roux is that chopped vegetables are cooked in the fat before the roux is made. The fat used for the brown sauce may be strongly flavoured (for instance dripping or bacon fat) rather than mildly flavoured.

When flour is added, the roux of flour and fat is cooked until nut brown, before the addition of liquid. The liquid used will be richer in colour and more strongly flavoured; it may be stock from red meat or game, or jellied beef stock from meat bones.

Stock

A well-flavoured stock is essential for a good brown sauce. The better the stock, the better the flavour of the finished sauce. For a simple brown sauce, a light vegetable stock or a bouillon cube can be used in an emergency, but jus lié, sauce espagnole and a demi-glace all need high quality beef stock.

The meat juices strained from a

Some of the ingredients required to make simple brown sauces.

pot-au-feu (meat stewed in liquid for hours to provide a broth) can be used for the brown stock used to make a simple sauce or a sauce espagnole; this will give excellent results. However for the demi-glace, the addition should be jellied brown stock (called fond brun) made from meat bones and then carefully skimmed of fat as described in the stock chapter.

Fats

For a brown roux, the fat may be dripping, oil, clarified butter or a mixture of butter and oil. Butter gives a good flavour but burns easily unless clarified; you can add a small quantity of oil to the butter to counteract this.

To make clarified butter, melt it in a small heavy-based pan and cook gently without allowing it to colour. Skim off with a metal spoon any scum or impurities that rise to the surface. Strain through a small strainer lined with muslin into a small bowl with a lip. Let the butter settle, then pour it into a second bowl leaving impurities behind.

For a sauce espagnole bacon is used, which supplies a proportion of the fat as well as lending its individual flavour. Salt pork may also be used or a proportion of diced ham substituted to provide the meat flavour.

Flours

For a brown roux, plain white flour is used. However this would not give a smooth enough result for a jus lié.

For jus lié, cornflour or arrowroot are used to give a clear sauce when cooked. Plain flour cannot be used as cooking time is insufficient.

Vegetable additions

Chopped vegetables are cooked in the fat before the flour is added. In the case of simple sauce, these are normally onion and carrot.

For sauce espagnole a selection of vegetables includes onion, carrot and celery, in balanced quantities so that no one flavour predominates. When the chopped bacon (or salt pork) is added to these chopped vegetables the whole is known as a mirepoix.

Mushroom peelings may also be included at this point. Mushroom peelings are often mentioned in recipes; this dates from an age when mushrooms were regularly peeled, and their skins were a common by-product in kitchens. These were always used by the economical French housewife. Nowadays mushroom stalks are the best choice. As a rough guide use the stalks from 225 g [½ lb] open (not button) mushrooms to make 250 ml [½ pt] sauce.

Tomatoes are added to the sauce

espagnole in the second stage. The sieve may be used to remove the skins and seeds from the sauce after cooking.

All the vegetables strained from the sauce after simmering have lost most of their flavour; they can therefore add little in this respect to another dish. However they may be added for bulk to, for example, a shepherds pie or a bolognese sauce.

Seasonings

As the flavour of the stock plays an important part in the making of a brown sauce, the first step is tc taste the stock. Its flavour will influence any further choice of seasoning.

If you are preparing the stock especially with a view to making a brown sauce, omit the salt. The long simmering and reduction process concentrates the seasonings which can become excessive—indeed it is a good idea always to reduce or omit salt from stock, as this can be better added with the final seasonings.

In a sauce espagnole, a bouquet garni of herbs is used. This consists of parsley, thyme and a bay leaf.

Seasoning and herbs are generally added to the completed sauce to give it character and individuality, and so these additions may better be considered as part of the subject of derivative sauces. It is in your selection and judgement of quantities of herbs and seasoning that you can give individuality to your cooking, so that it is worth experimenting with their flavours.

Garlic is used too, in brown sauces, but it should be used with discretion.

BROWN-ROUX SAUCE

A brown roux is made by cooking a small amount of finely chopped vegetables in the fat until they are just coloured. The flour is then added and the mixture cooked until it is a rich nut brown.

When making the sauce, you must bear in mind the following points.
● Always measure the fat and flour accurately. Fat may exceed flour according to the recipe, but never the other way round.
● Do not allow the fat to become so hot that it fries the vegetables, but let them cook slowly over medium-low heat for 5-10 minutes, stirring now and again.
● Add the flour off the medium-low heat, then stir the roux steadily all the time with a wooden spoon over the heat, so that it cooks to an even nut-brown colour. This will take 5-10 minutes. Never use a high heat and do not allow the roux to burn because this gives a bitter taste to the sauce. It will also prevent the flour from thickening the sauce. If the roux burns by accident, throw it away and start again.
● The stock should be cold or warm but never very hot when added. Take the pan off the heat before stirring in the stock. Then stir over heat until thickened.
● Simmer the sauce half covered. The heat should be as low as possible, so that the surface of the sauce only shows a movement in one place. It is the gentle reduction of the sauce and concentration of the flavours that gives the sauce its consistency and excellent flavour.
● If the sauce evaporates and becomes too thick during cooking, it can be thinned with a little more stock. If there is no more stock available, you can use water as the flavours will have concentrated.

Step-by-step to making jus lié

◨ *Unlike other brown sauces, jus lié does not have a roux as its base, but is a meat juice thickened by a liaison. A good quality brown stock is therefore essential. This is the quickest of all brown sauces to make.*

MAKES 250 ML [½ PT]
250 ml [½ pt] beef stock
15 g [½ oz] cornflour or 7 g [¼ oz] arrowroot

1 In a medium-sized mixing bowl, mix the starch with 30 ml [2 tablespoons] of the cold stock, stirring until blended.

Step-by-step to making simple brown sauce

MAKES 250 ML [½ PT]
1 small carrot
1 small onion
20 g [¾ oz] dripping or 30 ml [2 tablespoons] oil or 15 ml [1 tablespoon] oil and 15 g [½ oz] butter
20 g [¾ oz] flour
400 ml [¾ pt] beef stock
salt and black pepper

4 Remove pan from heat and stir in flour. Return to heat and stir for 5-10 minutes until nut brown.

5 Remove pan from heat and trickle in cool stock. Stir vigorously at first to blend evenly and smoothly.

2 Put the stock in a small heavy-based saucepan. Place over medium heat, and bring slowly to boiling point.

3 Remove pan from the heat and gradually pour the hot liquid into the starch mixture, stirring continuously until blended.

4 Return the sauce to the pan and boil, stirring, over medium heat for 3 minutes for cornflour or 1 minute for arrowroot. Season.

1 Wash and chop the carrot. Peel the onion and chop it finely. Measure the fat.

2 Melt or heat the fat over medium-low heat in a heavy-based pan about 15 cm [6"] diameter.

3 Add the vegetables and cook, stirring, for 5-10 minutes until they begin to brown.

6 Bring to the boil, stirring all the time. Half cover, reduce heat and simmer slowly for 45 minutes.

7 During simmering, periodically skim off fat. Add a little cold stock to help fat rise to the surface.

8 Strain, taste and season. Then reheat and serve, or use as the basis for another sauce.

• Never thicken a thin sauce by adding more flour at the last moment or it will taste of raw starch. To reduce it place the sauce in an uncovered pan over a high heat and boil until the consistency is right.

Degreasing
During the simmering process, you must skim off from time to time any scum or fat which rises to the surface of the sauce with a metal spoon. If the sauce still appears greasy, this may be corrected by adding a very small quantity of cold stock—about 45 ml [3 tablespoons] in two or three parts to the simmering sauce. This will encourage the grease to rise to the surface so that it may be easily skimmed off. This is called to 'dépouiller' a sauce—the French word meaning 'to skin'.

If the sauce is to be allowed to get cold, for storage or reheating later, any grease will set on top and can then be easily removed.

SERVING AND QUANTITIES
When planning to make a brown sauce, the first point to remember is that there should only be one rich sauce at a meal. You will be wasting your time, if you strive to create an effect by including more than one.

The amount of sauce should be small in proportion to the food. The meat (or dish) should not be swimming in so much sauce that it is necessary to take a spoon to it, but portions simply should be generously coated. When serving a sauce with grilled or sautéed meat, the meat is dished, coated with an average of 30 ml [2 tablespoons] per person. The remaining sauce is served in a sauce-boat.

For four people, 250 ml [½pt] is ample. Never be tempted to exceed this quantity; the result would be 'trop de richesse'.

Make a good quantity of sauce while you are at it. It takes no more time than a smaller quantity and can be stored to save you time on another day.

KEEPING AND REHEATING A BROWN SAUCE
A brown sauce may be kept hot and reheated in exactly the same way as a white sauce. If you intend to reheat the sauce, place a circle of buttered

greaseproof paper over the surface when hot.

To reheat the sauce, place it in a double boiler or bain-marie. To prevent lumps forming, raise the temperature of the sauce gradually, by bringing the water in the outer pan slowly to the boil. Whisk the sauce while it is reheating with a sauce whisk. Strain the sauce after heating if this is necessary.

If you wish to make a derivative sauce proceed to make additions at this point.

STORING
All the basic brown sauces keep well, so it is worth always making them in larger quantities than will be eaten at one meal. And any of these four can be stored for at least a week in a covered jar in the refrigerator, but should be brought to the boil again after four days. Allow the sauce to cool, then replace it in its covered jar.

Brown sauces can also be frozen satisfactorily and stored for a month in the freezer. It is most convenient to freeze the prepared sauce in 150 or 275 ml [¼ or ½ pt] quantities. Freeze in measured containers then wrap individually in foil before placing in freezer bags or plastic containers for storage. You can then make instant use of the right amount, reheating the quantity you need for any particular dish.

ESPAGNOLE SAUCE
This is a sophisticated version of the simple brown sauce. More vegetables are used, while the mushroom stalks give the sauce a good colour and flavour. Bacon is added to the fat for extra flavour. Chopped ham may be substituted for the bacon as this makes the sauce less greasy without detracting from the flavour.

After the roux has been made, the sauce is simmered for an hour to concentrate its flavours. Chopped tomatoes are then added, and further simmering takes place. It is this long reduction, two hours cooking time in all, that clarifies the sauce and concentrates its flavours.

Espagnole sauce stores well, so it is advisable always to make double the quantity needed for one meal. This recipe will give you enough for two meals for four people, or one such meal plus enough to make demi-glace for four.

MAKES 550 ML [1 PT]
1 medium-sized carrot
1 stick celery
1 medium-sized onion
25 g [1 oz] mushroom stalks
50 g [2 oz] streaky bacon or ham
40 g [1½ oz] dripping or 25 g [1oz] butter and 15 ml [1 tablespoon] oil or 40 g [1½ oz] clarified butter
40 g [1½ oz] plain flour
675 ml [1¼ pt] good beef stock
1 bouquet garni
225 g [½ lb] tomatoes or 10 ml [2 teaspoons] tomato purée
salt and pepper

1 Wash the carrot and celery, peel the onion, remove the earthy ends from the mushroom stalks and chop all the vegetables.

2 Rind and dice the bacon or ham. Melt the fat in a medium-sized heavy-based saucepan over medium heat and add the bacon, if using. Cook bacon for a minute.

3 Add the chopped vegetables and the ham, if using, to the fat. Cook gently until they begin to colour.

4 Add the flour off the heat, then cook for 5-10 minutes, stirring, until it is a rich nut brown.

5 Remove from the heat and gradually add the stock, stirring continually. Return to the heat and bring to the boil, stirring all the while.

6 Add the bouquet garni, half cover and simmer slowly for 1 hour.

7 During simmering, skim from time to time with a metal spoon. Three times add 15 ml [1 tablespoon] cold stock or water to precipitate the fat to the surface of the liquid, then skim the fat off.

8 Meanwhile, if using tomatoes, chop them and add them, or the tomato purée, to the hot sauce.

9 Half cover and simmer for a further ¾ hour. The tomatoes, if used, will reduce to a pulp and the sauce will further reduce.

10 Strain the sauce through a fine sieve into a bowl, pressing all the juices from the vegetables. Discard the vegetables.

11 If serving a proportion of the sauce immediately, rinse out the pan and pour back the quantity needed. Season to taste, reheat and serve.

12 For storing, season the sauce to taste in the bowl. Allow to become cold, cover and transfer to the refrigerator and subsequently to the freezer if wished.

DEMI-GLACE SAUCE

◪◪ *Of the four basic brown sauces, this is the richest and the most flavourful—one of the glories of French cuisine. It is a good sauce to serve with sautéed tournedos, roast pheasant or partridge or, more often, with sautéed chicken. Sauces derived from it are also superb.*
Make the sauce espagnole following the previous recipe, steps 1-10.

MAKES 250 ml [½ pt]
250 ml [½ pt] espagnole sauce
150 ml [¼ pt] jellied beef stock

1 Put the sauce espagnole in a medium-sized heavy-based saucepan. Add the jellied beef stock and simmer until the sauce has reduced by one third to 250 ml [½ pt], about 30 minutes.

2 Adjust seasoning and serve. However, if you intend to use this sauce as the base for another, either allow to cool and reserve, or proceed immediately, as planned.

DERIVATIVE SAUCES

As well as being served to make dishes in their own right, the four basic brown sauces can be used to make other sauces. Basically the derivative sauces are made by adding extra ingredients to the mother sauce before serving.

Any one of the four sauces mères can be used. Examples of sauces derived from simple brown sauce are cider sauce and sauce lyonnaise.

However the majority of derivative sauces are made either from espagnole or demi-glace. Examples of the first are chasseur, bourguignonne and bigarade. Examples of the second are romaine, à la diable, fines herbes and rouennaise.

The best results are obtained from the two best quality sauces, espagnole and demi-glace. It would really be a waste of money to make an expensive addition to a simple sauce—to try, for example, to make a Périgueux sauce by addition truffles to a simple brown sauce.

Many of the sauces are double derivatives, setting aside for the moment the fact that demi-glace is itself made from espagnole.

A Périgueux sauce is made by adding truffles to a sauce madère, which is itself made by adding Madeira to an espagnole. A venaison is made by adding redcurrant jelly and cream to a poivrade, which is itself made by adding red wine and juniper berries to a simple brown roux.

Cider sauce,
based on a simple
brown sauce, is a
tasty choice for gammon steaks.

Ingredients for derivative sauces

The choice of additions to make an individual sauce is extremely wide. This will depend on the dish of which it is to form part, the amount of time and sometimes money that you want to spend on it, available ingredients and lastly your own personal inspiration. Additions can be divided roughly into groups.

Vegetable or fruit additions: onions and other chopped vegetables may be added. These are invariably cooked before the addition is made. This may be by softening in butter or they may be simmered in liquid, usually wine. Oranges and frequently citrus zest are added to brown sauces.

Vinegars, alcohol and wines: red or white wine, cider, brandy or red- or white-wine vinegar all make successful additions. Alcoholic liquors and vinegar are invariably reduced before being added to the sauce mère.

Herbs and spices: fresh herbs are often added. These may be simmered in the sauce and then strained before serving or they may be added to the final dish. Cinnamon, nutmeg, mace, all peppers and Worcestershire sauce, all play a part.

Mustard, jelly and cream: mustard may be added to a finished sauce, or gooseberry or, more often, red-current jelly melted in it. Cream may be added to a brown sauce and heated through before serving.

Sugar: sugar may be cooked to a pale caramel and used as an addition.

Poultry livers: these may be cooked, pounded and then added.
Final garnishes: chopped items such as gherkins and capers may be added to a finished sauce.

Experimenting for yourself

The classic combinations are famous, but you will find there are several versions of the same sauce, giving different proportions of the same or similar ingredients. Most of the great French chefs have left their own version of a classic sauce. Try out some of the classic recipes and then experiment on your own. Think of the details and do not be afraid to improvise.

Planning forward

The prospect of making a sauce in order to make another sauce may seem daunting, but it is not really so, though it does require a little kitchen planning. You will soon come to regard it as an advantage to be 'half way there' to another delicious meal.

For example, you might find yourself making the brown stock given in the chapter on stocks, because you have bought meat bones. You might then plan to serve sauce espagnole and reserve part. Make the espagnole in the double quantity given in the recipe, serve half of it for a coming meal and reserve the rest.

You then have the two necessary elements to make a superb demi-glace in about half an hour, and almost as quickly, you can make sauces derived from the demi-glace such as sauce madère.

SERVING SUGGESTIONS

Sophisticated sauces make simple ingredients into memorable meals. Try some of the following ideas, using 250 ml [½ pt] sauce or substitute other sauce from the chart.

- Grilled chicken is a dish to remember with a sauce à la diable.
- Reheat cold bacon or ham slices in cider sauce, or pour cider sauce over grilled gammon steaks.
- Serve boiled Jerusalem artichokes with sauce italienne and garnish with grilled bacon slices for a main dish.
- Try soft-boiled eggs with a coating of sauce fines herbs. Serve a generous border of croûtons round the dish to provide a contrast in textures.
- Serve grilled kidneys with a sauce madère.
- Turn new potatoes into a main dish by covering them with a sauce chasseur; serve a green vegetable with them.
- Sauce lyonnaise, quicker to make than many other brown sauces, will make fried liver taste more exciting.
- Poached eggs are delicious served on canapés coated with sauce bourguignonne.
- For a single-crust pie, combine left-over mutton with a proportion of carrots and a mustard sauce.
- Try romaine sauce with steamed whole small onions as an impressive side dish to roast pork.
- Serve tongue hot with the slices coated with sauce piquante.
- Sauce bigarade, excellent with duck, can also be served with roast mutton as a change from mint sauce. With the addition of diced ham, bigarade is also suitable for pasta.
- Add port to a demi-glace instead of Madeira and use with chicken livers to fill vol-au-vent.

Classic sauces made by the brown-roux method (serves 6)

Sauce	Additions	Method	Serve with
A la diable 250 ml [½pt] demi-glace sauce	25 g [1 oz] chopped shallots, 15 g [½ oz] butter, 125 ml [4 fl oz] brandy or 175 ml [6 fl oz] white wine. plus 15 ml [1 tablespoon] vinegar, 30 ml [2 tablespoons] tomato purée, 5 ml [1 teaspoon] each of chopped chervil, cayenne pepper, Worcestershire sauce.	Soften shallots in butter. Add brandy or wine plus vinegar. Reduce by boiling gently about 5-8 minutes to 50 ml [2 fl oz]. Add sauce and heat, then add tomato purée and chervil. Cook 5 min. Strain then add cayenne and Worcestershire sauce to taste.	Spicy sauce for grilled chicken and grilled meat.
Bigarade 250 ml [½ pt] espagnole sauce	50 g [2 oz] chopped shallots, 25 g [1 oz] butter, 2 Seville oranges, or 1 orange and 1 lemon, 175 ml [6 fl oz] red wine, 15 ml [1 tablespoon] redcurrent jelly.	Soften shallots in butter. Meanwhile pare zest from 1 orange, make julienne strips and blanche and refresh these twice. Squeeze citrus fruit and add juice, red wine and julienne strips to shallots. Reduce by boiling gently to 50 ml [2 fl oz] about 8 min. Heat the sauce and add wine mix and redcurrent jelly. Simmer 5 min. until jelly has melted and blended, strain if wished and serve.	Duck
Bourguignonne 250 ml [½ pt] espagnole sauce	25 g [1 oz] shallots, 15 g [½ oz] butter, 550 ml [1 pt] red wine, bouquet garni.	Sweat shallots in butter. Add red wine and herbs and boil gently for 25 minutes to reduce to 150 ml [4 fl oz]. Add sauce and boil gently to reduce to 350 ml [12 fl oz] about 5 min. Strain and serve.	Red meat, sautéed poultry (make in sauté pan), poached eggs.
Chasseur 250 ml [½ pt] espagnole sauce	50 g [2 oz] chopped shallots, 40 g [1½ oz] butter, 100 g [4 oz] mushrooms, 175 ml [6 fl oz] white wine, 100 g [4 oz] tomatoes or 15 ml [1 tablespoon] tomato purée, 15 ml [1 tablespoon] chopped parsley.	Soften shallots in butter and add finely sliced mushrooms. Cook 2 minutes. Add white wine and boil gently about 8 min. to reduce 50 ml [2 fl oz]. Add peeled, deseeded, chopped tomatoes, cook 10 min. Add sauce then tomato purée if using. Add chopped parsley and serve.	Sautéed chicken, rabbit, grilled noisettes of lamb, noodles.
Cider 250 ml [½ pt] simple brown sauce.	150 ml [¼ pt] dry cider, ½ bay leaf, ½ clove.	Put cider, bay leaf and clove in pan. Boil gently until reduced to 50 ml [2 fl oz], about 5 min. Add sauce, simmer 5 minutes, strain and serve.	Sliced boiled bacon and ham.
Fines herbes 250 ml [½ pt] demi-glace sauce	175 ml [6 fl oz] white wine, 5 ml [1 teaspoon] each tarragon, chervil, chives, parsley, 5 ml [1 teaspoon] lemon juice.	Bring wine to boil, add herbs and boil 8 min. to reduce to 50 ml [2 fl oz]. Add sauce and lemon juice, simmer 5 min. then strain. Add extra chopped herbs if liked, then serve. For a tarragon sauce add 45 ml [3 tablespoons] tarragon.	Eggs, fish, a binding sauce.

Classic sauces made by the brown-roux method (serves 6)

Sauce	Additions	Method	Serve with
Italienne 250 ml [½ pt] demi-glace sauce	15 g [½ oz] butter, 50 g [2 oz] mushrooms, 50 g [2 oz] chopped ham, 25 g [1 oz] chopped onion, 150 ml [¼ pt] white wine, 15 ml [1 tablespoon] tomato purée, 10 ml [2 teaspoons] parsley.	Soften mushrooms in butter, add ham and onion. Cook gently 3-4 min. Add wine and boil gently for 5 min. to reduce to 50 ml [2 fl oz]. Add sauce and tomato purée and heat through. Add parsley.	Excellent with pasta, root vegetables such as celeriac.
Lyonnaise 250 ml [½ pt] simple brown sauce	50 g [2 oz] chopped onion, 15 g [½ oz] butter, 50 ml [2 fl oz] white wine, 50 ml [2 fl oz] white wine vinegar.	Soften onions in butter. Add wine and vinegar and boil gently 5 min. to reduce to 50 ml [2 fl oz]. Add sauce, simmer 15 min. Strain or serve with onions.	Liver, meat and vegetables.
Madère 250 ml [½ pt] demi-glace sauce	125 ml [4 fl oz] Madeira wine	Boil the Madeira gently until it has reduced by half, about 5 min. Add the sauce and simmer another 5 min.	Veal escalopes, meat and game.
Mustard 250 ml [½ pt] demi-glace sauce	50 g [2 oz] chopped onion, 25 g [1 oz] butter, 175 ml [6 oz] white wine, thyme, bay leaf, 10 ml [2 teaspoons] Dijon mustard, 5 ml [1 teaspoon] lemon juice.	Sweat onions in butter. Add wine and herbs. Boil about 8 min. to reduce to 50 ml [2 fl oz]. Add sauce and simmer 5 min. Strain then add mustard and lemon juice.	Grilled bacon, pork and ham.
Robert 250 ml [½ pt] demi-glace sauce	25 g [1 oz] onion, 25 g [1 oz] butter, 125 ml [4 fl oz] white wine, 20 ml [4 teaspoons] French mustard, 25 g [1 oz] gherkins, 5 ml [1 teaspoon] parsley.	Sweat the onion in the butter. Add the wine and boil gently for 5 min. until reduced to 50 ml [2 fl oz]. Add sauce and simmer 10 min. Strain if wished. Add mustard, gherkins and parsley.	Roast pork, grilled chops, kidneys.
Romaine 250 ml [½ pt] demi-glace sauce	30 ml [2 tablespoons] granulated sugar, 175 ml [6 fl oz] wine vinegar, 50 g [2 oz] sultanas.	Allow sugar to dissolve over gentle heat without stirring and to colour brown. Remove from heat and stir in vinegar. Reduce this by boiling gently until the sugar is on the point of caramelizing again, about 10 min. Add sauce and sultanas. Barely simmer until sultanas plump up.	Tongue, venison, beef, braised mutton.
Rouennaise 250 ml [½ pt] demi-glace sauce	25 g [1 oz] onions, 65 g [2½ oz] butter, 175 ml [6 fl oz] red wine, 175 g [6 oz] ducks' or chickens' livers.	Soften onions in 25 g [1 oz] butter. Add the wine and boil gently to reduce to 25 ml [1 fl oz], about 10 min. Dice the livers and cook them gently in the rest of the butter in another pan, this will take 6-8 min. Add a little of the demi-glace to the livers, then reduce them to a purée in a liquidizer or through a sieve. Add the rest of the demi-glace and the purée to the reduced wine, and heat.	Duck.

Loin chops
with sauce Robert

Star recipe

★

LOIN CHOPS WITH SAUCE ROBERT

These grilled pork chops are lifted from the ordinary and made dinner party fare by the sharp-tasting sauce, made from a demi-glace sauce. If you have sauce espagnole stored in the refrigerator, you can start at step 8 and the recipe will take you three-quarters of an hour. Serve with new potatoes.

SERVES 4
4 loin pork chops
30 ml [2 tablespoons] oil

For the demi-glace sauce:
40 g [1½ oz] butter
1 small carrot
1 celery stick
1 small onion
25 g [1 oz] mushroom stalks
50 g [2 oz] streaky bacon
1 bouquet garni
675 ml [1¼ pt] good brown stock
10 ml [2 teaspoon] tomato purée
salt and black pepper
150 ml [¼ pt] jellied brown stock

For the sauce Robert:
1 small onion
25 g [1 oz] butter
125 ml [4 fl oz] white wine
25 g [1 oz] gherkins
20 ml [4 teaspoons]
 French mustard
5 ml [1 teaspoon] chopped
 parsley

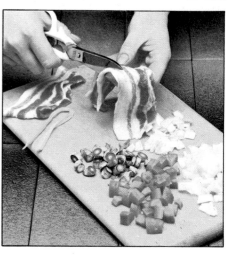

1 Wash the carrot and celery, peel onion, chop with mushrooms. Remove bacon rind and chop.

5 Remove from the heat and trickle in the brown stock, stirring continuously. Bring to the boil.

6 Add the bouquet garni, cover and simmer for 1 hour. Skim off any fat that rises with a skimming spoon.

7 Add a spoonful of cold stock. Let the fat rise to surface and skim off. Do this again. Add tomato purée.

11 Turn grill to highest heat and arrange the chops in single layer in gratin dish.

12 Continue the sauce. Peel and chop onion. Melt butter in small heavy-based pan; cook onion till soft.

13 Add the wine and simmer to reduce by half. Add to demi-glace; simmer for 20 minutes.

2 Melt butter in a medium-sized heavy-based pan. Add the bacon and sweat for 2 minutes.

3 Add the vegetables and cook over low heat until onion softens. Stir occasionally.

4 Add flour off the heat, then cook, stirring all the time, until the roux is a rich nut brown.

8 Strain the sauce through a sieve, into a small saucepan, pressing all the juices from the vegetables.

9 Add the jellied stock. Simmer until the sauce has reduced to 250 ml [½ pt] about 30 minutes.

10 Brush the loin chops on both sides with a little of the oil. Set aside till ready to cook.

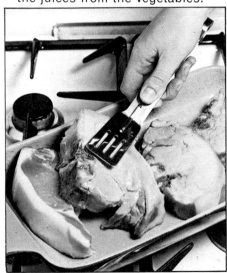

14 Grill chops 1 minute each side. Lower heat or dish and grill 5-7 minutes each side, basting.

15 Chop gherkins. When sauce is ready, stir in mustard, gherkins and parsley. Do not reheat.

16 Dish pork chops on to warmed serving dish. Spoon a little sauce over each portion of meat.

Sauces

mayonnaise and emulsion sauces

Creating a smooth, home-made mayonnaise by combining egg yolks and oil seems more like a conjuring trick than cookery. This course shows you just how to get the trick right and how to flavour and use mayonnaise in exciting ways.

Sauces made with egg yolks are rich and, classic. There are two types of 'emulsion' sauce, as it is known. For the first type, egg yolks are combined with oil and seasonings, without cooking, and the result is a mayonnaise. The second type of emulsion sauce is based on egg yolks and butter, which are gently cooked together: the results are called fine butter sauces or hollandaise and these are described in detail in the next chapter.

MAYONNAISE AND ITS USES

Mayonnaise is the most famous and indispensable of cold sauces. Egg yolks and oil plus flavourings are blended together very carefully and gradually so the yolks hold in the other ingredients in creamy suspension. This glossy rich sauce has innumerable uses.

The basic mayonnaise acts as a spring-board for many other sauces, by the addition of fresh herbs and spices, tangy gherkins, anchovies and capers, colourful vegetable purées and refreshing fruit juices. Mixed with aspic jelly, mayonnaise becomes a mayonnaise collée for

creating chaudfroids (which are used for coating cold meats).

A mayonnaise is one of the most adaptable of sauces. It is marvellous for dressing-up pieces of cold cooked chicken, salmon, turkey, ham or lobster—and can turn humbler foods such as simple poached cod or haddock into something special. It goes well with small amounts of left-over vegetables (that might otherwise be destined for the bin) which are diced and bound together by a creamy rich mayonnaise mixture to make the classic Russian and potato salads.

Hard-boiled eggs coated with a rich mayonnaise make one of the simplest, quickest and most attractive of all hors d'oeuvres. Mixed with prawns, shrimps or crab and a few seasonings, mayonnaise forms the basis of a seafood cocktail.

Even the very best commercially produced mayonnaises are an in-

A flawlessly smooth mayonnaise is the classic accompaniment to poached salmon steaks.

ferior copy of the real thing. On no account should the commercially marketed 'salad cream' be used in the place of mayonnaise—it is not the same thing.

INGREDIENTS

The main ingredients are eggs and oil and it is important to use the correct proportions.

Eggs

It is important that the egg yolks used in mayonnaise are fresh—stale yolks may curdle the mixture. Large egg yolks are the best to use. The maximum amount of oil a large yolk will absorb is 175 ml [6 fl oz]. If you attempt to exceed this, it's a guaranteed failure, as the binding properties of the yolk will collapse, and the sauce will thin out or curdle. For beginners 125 ml [4 fl oz] is the sensible amount of oil to use, 150 ml [$\frac{1}{4}$ pt] once you are confident.

A basic mayonnaise recipe usually gives 250 ml [$\frac{1}{2}$ pt] oil for 2 egg yolks, the addition of a third yolk makes a thicker sauce.

Some sauces in the mayonnaise family use cooked egg yolks. The hard-boiled yolks are pushed through a sieve and the mayonnaise made in the usual way. This gives the mayonnaise a different consistency and characteristic taste. This type of sauce cannot be made in a liquidizer. Cooked egg yolks will hold the oil in the same way as raw ones, but need a smaller quantity, about 50 ml [2 fl oz] per large egg yolk.

Flavourings

Ready-made French, dry or ready-made English mustard can be used according to taste, but usually 2.5 ml [$\frac{1}{2}$ teaspoon] each of mustard and salt are used to every 250 ml [$\frac{1}{2}$ pt] oil. Salt is essential, but pepper is a rarer addition. Season with 1.5 ml [$\frac{1}{4}$ teaspoon] white pepper as black pepper will spoil the look of the mayonnaise.

Oil

The main flavouring of mayonnaise is oil and some recipes state that only olive oil should be used. In fact, olive oil used by itself is too strong for many palates, particularly if you are not accustomed to its fruity flavour. Olive oil is also very expensive, even when bought in bulk, so that a mixture of olive oil with one of the vegetable oils, such as corn oil, is more economical. The blander flavour of the resulting mayonnaise is preferred by many people. Use half olive oil, half corn oil for a less potent flavour, and 25 per cent olive oil, 75 per cent corn oil for economy.

Vinegar

Almost any vinegar can be used according to taste, except malt vinegar; the flavour of this is too strong for a mayonnaise. White-wine vinegar is the most frequently used, but try ringing the changes and find out what suits your palate by using a herb vinegar such as tarragon, or cider or garlic vinegar.

Lemon juice can replace vinegar in the same proportions—essential for a lemon-flavoured mayonnaise.

EQUIPMENT

The only equipment you need is an ordinary mixing bowl and a wooden spoon. However, you could use a wire balloon whisk or an electric whisk instead of a spoon—or even a liquidizer. This method is different (see liquidizer method).

It is important to be comfortable when making mayonnaise by hand, so choose a bowl which is large enough to move the spoon about in easily. Place the bowl on a damp tea-towel so it will stay put, leaving both your hands free to make the mayonnaise.

It's helpful, too, to have a measuring jug for the oil and a spoon for the lemon juice or vinegar, because it is important that the right quantities are used and that oil is added slowly. A method recommended for beginners which is even easier than pouring from a jug is to fill a bottle with the right amount of oil and then make two V-shaped notches in opposite sides of the cork stopper. The oil drops from the lower groove, while air enters the bottle from the upper groove, so that a slow measured pace is ensured.

THE BASIC METHOD

Many cooks (even experienced ones) are apprehensive of making mayonnaise, because they are afraid that it will curdle. It is undoubtedly a delicate job, but not very difficult once you understand the processes involved. Then, as long as you follow a few simple rules given here, the whole operation will go smoothly. After you have made mayonnaise a couple of times, you should confidently be able to make 550 ml [1 pt] mayonnaise in less than 10 minutes.

Incidentally, if you want to make larger quantities, it is probably better to make several batches, each using three or four yolks, rather than to make one huge batch using, for example, 12 yolks!

Principles and initial preparation

Basically, the process of making mayonnaise involves coaxing egg yolks into absorbing oil and, once absorbed, to hold it in suspension. This 'marriage' is achieved by having both oil and yolks at the same temperature or what might be described as 'in a receptive mood'.

Both eggs and oil should be allowed to stand at room temperature for one hour before making the mayonnaise. If you forget to allow time for this, cloudy and chilled olive oil can be made clear again by

Mayonnaise is created from egg yolks and oil, w

standing the bottle in a basin of warm water for a few minutes. Whole eggs in their shells can be immersed in tepid water, too, or gently warmed under a tap until room temperature is reached.

A warm mixing bowl will also help create the right atmosphere for the blending. Dip it in hot water, dry and place it firmly on a damp tea-towel.

Even after these precautions have been taken, the eggs need further encouragement to make them ready to welcome the oil. This is done by beating them for a minute or two to make them smooth, thick and sticky.

The next thing is to blend seasonings into the yolks—salt, mustard and vinegar or lemon juice (usually no more than 15 ml [1 tablespoon] of vinegar per two egg yolks at this stage). A little acid helps the oil to blend with the yolks. Blend the yolks in gently but firmly taking the wooden spoon or whisk round the sides and base of the bowl so they are well mixed. When the mixture is creamy, it is ready for the oil.

Incorporating the oil

Providing the preparations described above have been carried out, and the oil has been carefully measured, you should have no trouble in affecting the marriage. It is essential to introduce the oil to the yolks very slowly, particularly at first.

Hold the jug or bottle in your left hand and the spoon (or electric whisk) in your right—or vice versa if you are left handed. Rest the lip on the edge of the bowl and pour just one drop of oil on to the seasoned yolks beating it in with the spoon as you pour.

The beating should be fast but not furious (about two strokes per second) round the whole bowl to incorporate the oil evenly. After a few seconds, still beating, add a second drop of oil and blend it in. Continue beating in the oil, drop by drop, until the mixture starts to form a thick yellow paste. You can change hands, or change directions of beating, but you must not stop until the mixture has thickened.

It is very important not to rush the beginning; the yolks cannot absorb much oil at a time—and this is particularly true at the beginning. Never attempt to add another drop of oil until you are sure the previous one has been properly incorporated into the mixture. For the same reason, adding a fast trickle instead of a drop or two of oil before the oil is absorbed could cause curdling. So keep calm and do things slowly—in fact, you cannot add the oil too slowly.

Adding oil at the second stage

When the mixture is very thick and creamy and about one-third to one-half of the oil has been used up your success is assured. You can now rest a moment; the crisis point has passed.

It is now safe to start adding the remaining oil in a slow but steady trickle. Continue beating all the time as at the first stage. Every few moments stop trickling in the oil to double check that the oil is still being absorbed by the yolks and is not flowing too fast.

If the mayonnaise becomes so thick that beating is difficult and your wrists begin to ache, stop adding the oil. Beat in a little more lemon or vinegar before continuing. This will thin the mixture and make it easier to handle. Taste the mixture and if you think it is already sufficiently sharp use 15 ml [1 tablespoon] of water instead.

Finishing touches

When all the oil has been absorbed by the yolks, the mayonnaise should be the consistency of thick whipped cream. It will hold its shape when the spoon is lifted from the mixture and will drop with a slow plop back into the bowl.

blended together with seasonings of mustard, salt and pepper to form a glossy rich sauce.

Step-by-step to making mayonnaise

2 large-sized egg yolks
2.5 ml [½ teaspoon] French or English mustard
2.5 ml [½ teaspoon] salt
15 ml [1 tablespoon] vinegar or lemon juice
250 ml [½ pt] olive oil or 50% olive, 50% corn oil

1 Assemble the equipment and the ingredients at least one hour before making the mayonnaise.

OR warm the eggs by immersing in warm water and the oil by standing in a jug of warm water.

3 Add mustard, salt, vinegar or lemon juice and beat with spoon or whisk for further ½ minute.

4 Rest lip of bottle with notched cork on edge of bowl and hold the whisk in your other hand.

5 Add the first drop of oil. Beat right round the sides and base until completely incorporated.

7 When mixture is thick, the crisis is over, so rest if necessary. Then start a steady trickle of oil.

8 Keep beating. If mayonnaise becomes too thick, thin with a little lemon juice, vinegar or water.

9 The finished mayonnaise should hold its shape, and drop from the spoon or beaters with a plop.

2 Warm bowl in hot water, dry, stand on cloth, add yolks and beat 1-2 minutes until thick and sticky.

6 When it is absorbed add the next drop. Never stop beating—change hands if necessary.

10 Beat in 15-30 ml [1-2 tablespoons] boiling water. Taste for seasonings, adding pepper if liked.

As a final insurance against separating, beat 15-30 ml [1-2 tablespoons] boiling water into the sauce. This is usually done if the mayonnaise is to be refrigerated before use. Taste to check seasonings and blend in more salt, vinegar or lemon juice if wished. Pepper is rarely used but can be added. Use freshly ground white pepper; black pepper would spoil the glossy smooth appearance.

CURING CURDLED MAYONNAISE

Curdling is usually the result of adding oil too rapidly in the initial stages, but it can be corrected. If the oil and egg show signs of separating try adding a few drops of cold water and beating very hard. This will only be successful if you catch the mayonnaise at the very first signs of curdling.

If the mayonnaise curdles completely, there are three methods of correction. They are all based on the principle of starting with a new emulsion and then adding to it the curdled mayonnaise, so that it emulsifies again.

Using a new egg yolk

Starting again with one fresh egg yolk is the most expensive method of curing curdled mayonnaise. Place the yolk in a clean bowl (which should be at room temperature) beat, then slowly pour the curdled mixture on to the egg, beating well between each addition. The mayonnaise will become very thick because of the extra yolk. To thin it down a little, beat a few drops of lemon juice or water into the final mayonnaise.

Using mustard

Warm a mixing bowl and put in 5 ml [1 teaspoon] of made mustard. Beat in 15 ml [1 tablespoon] mayonnaise, using a whisk. When the two are blended, gradually add the rest of the curdled mayonnaise, no more than 15 ml [1 teaspoon] at a time. This is a laborious method, but is sure to work and cheaper than adding an egg yolk.

Using a bread paste

The Italians soak a tiny bit of white crustless bread in water and pulp it down with a spoon until it looks like a thick cream (about 5 ml [1 teaspoon]). Then gradually blend in the sauce as previously described.

LIQUIDIZER METHOD

If you're nervous of failure when making a mayonnaise by hand, here is a foolproof method that is also quick and easy.

A mayonnaise can be made in a matter of minutes in a liquidizer. Even one-speed liquidizers will blend the mayonnaise without curdling. Ingredients are used in the same quantities—with one important exception. Most liquidizer blades are fixed too high above the base of the goblet to whip two egg yolks effectively. So (unless you plan to make large amounts of mayonnaise) use whole eggs, allowing one whole large egg per scant 250 ml [½ pt] of oil.

Made in this way, the mayonnaise does not have the same golden rich colour—it is much thinner and lighter, but it is certainly far better than the commercial type. An advantage of liquidizer mayonnaise is that it keeps successfully several days longer in the fridge than the traditional sort.

Place the whole eggs and seasonings in the liquidizer goblet. Cover and blend for four seconds. For liquidizers with speed control, reduce the speed to moderate and add the oil in a thin, steady stream through the opening in the cover, until it is completely blended with the eggs.

If you are using a liquidizer with one (high) speed, add the oil to the liquidizer in batches, stopping to rest the blades occasionally. Adjust the seasonings.

STORING AND FREEZING

You will probably find it convenient to make at least 250 ml [½ pt] mayonnaise at a time.

If you have any remaining after use, turn into a small bowl or jar just large enough to take it. Cover with cling film or foil to prevent a skin forming and store in a cold larder or in the bottom of the refrigerator. Hand-made mayonnaise will keep for up to a week. Liquidizer mayonnaise will keep for several days longer. Do not stir before bringing it back to room temperature or there is a danger of the mayonnaise thinning out.

Mayonnaise cannot be frozen because the ingredients freeze at different temperatures and the sauce would curdle on thawing making it most unappetizing.

Mayonnaise Variations

Unless otherwise stated these amounts are based on the basic mayonnaise using 250 ml [½ pt] oil, and the flavourings are in addition to those already in the basic mayonnaise.

Sauce	Additions	Method	Serving suggestions
Mousseline	2 egg whites	Whisk egg whites until standing in peaks and fold into the mayonnaise.	An economic, fluffy mayonnaise to serve with cold, lightly cooked vegetables.
Chantilly	½ lemon, 45 ml [3 tablespoons] whipped cream.	Season with lemon juice and fold in the whipped cream.	Serve with cold asparagus.
Rémoulade	15 ml [1 tablespoon] chopped parsley, tarragon, chervil or basil, 1 clove garlic, 5 ml [1 teaspoon] chopped capers, 5 ml [1 teaspoon] dry mustard, 2 small gherkins, finely chopped, 2.5 ml [½ teaspoon] anchovy essence.	Crush the garlic. Mix all the ingredients together and fold into the mayonnaise. Chill and serve.	Serve with grilled fish, cold pork, prawns or shrimps.
Aioli	3-4 garlic cloves	This mayonnaise is made without initial seasonings of mustard, vinegar or lemon juice. Crush garlic with a little salt to a very smooth paste. Work into the egg yolks before adding oil as for basic mayonnaise. When complete, add lemon juice, salt and pepper to taste.	A traditional dish from Provence consisting of a dish of the sauce surrounded with a mixture of lightly cooked vegetables such as broad beans, French beans, carrots, potatoes baked in their skins, hard-boiled eggs and boiled beef. Also good with hot fish soups and boiled fish.
Mayonnaise verte	30 ml [2 tablespoons] frozen spinach, ½ bunch watercress leaves, 15 ml [1 tablespoon] parsley, a little fresh tarragon.	Place additions together in a pan with a little water. Simmer for 5-6 minutes. Drain, squeeze dry and purée. Fold into basic mayonnaise.	This is the traditional sauce to serve with cold salmon or salmon trout.
Gribiche	Replace raw egg yolks with 3 hard-boiled egg yolks, 15 ml [1 tablespoon] French mustard, 1-2 hard-boiled egg whites.	Use only 150 ml [¼ pt] oil. Sieve egg yolks, add seasonings and mustard, then work in the oil as for basic mayonnaise. Chop egg white finely and fold into finished sauce.	Serve with shellfish and cold fish. Also good with cold cooked vegetables and for raw vegetables such as crudités.
Tartare	Use 2 hard-boiled egg yolks and 1 raw egg yolk, 5 ml [1 teaspoon] each of finely chopped chives, parsley and capers, 1 small gherkin.	Sieve the hard-boiled egg yolks. Make the mayonnaise with the hard-boiled egg yolks mixed with raw egg yolk. Finely chop the gherkin and fold the gherkin with the remaining additions into the finished sauce.	Serve with fried or grilled fish, cold beef and cold chicken.

VARIATIONS AND DERIVATIVE SAUCES

Derivative sauces are made by stirring or folding additional ingredients into the mayonnaise, after it has been made, to give extra flavour.

The chart of derivative sauces, opposite, shows mayonnaise variations, including those based on hard-boiled rather than raw egg yolks.

Hard-boiled egg mayonnaise

This type of mayonnaise has a slightly different taste and consistency. It is less rich, because less oil per yolk is used.

To make this type of mayonnaise the eggs are hard boiled and the whites reserved. The yolks are sieved to produce a fine texture. They are then mixed to a smooth paste with flavourings and the oil is gradually blended in exactly as described in the step-by-step method, the only difference being that no more than 50 ml [2 fl oz] is used per yolk.

If hard-boiled egg whites are very finely chopped and added to the resulting mayonnaise, they give a light flavour and good body—just right for spooning over cold foods.

Dry flavourings

Making mayonnaise gives an excellent opportunity for you to experiment and find your own favourite flavourings. All the quantities given here are based on a basic mayonnaise made with 250 ml [½ pt] oil.

● Fresh herbs such as parsley, tarragon, chervil, basil and chives are classic additions. The French call this type of mayonnaise aux fines herbes. Herbs should be finely chopped—use about 15 ml [1 tablespoon]. Try experimenting with one of your favourite herbs, or a judicious mixture of two or more. Dried herbs should never be used.

● Stronger flavourings are generally added in smaller proportions. For a garlic-flavoured mayonnaise use one crushed garlic clove (this is different from the classic aioli).

● Add a sharp, tangy taste to mayonnaise with approximately 5 ml [1 teaspoon] chopped gherkins, capers or anchovies (or anchovy essence).

● Curry can also be added to mayonnaise. Curry paste is preferable to powder because the flavours blend better than powder, and although it is not strictly 'dry' it does not alter the consistency of the mayonnaise. Use up to 15 ml [1 tablespoon] curry paste, according to taste—delicious with pasta, salads and cold chicken or turkey.

Liquid flavourings

Liquid flavourings added to a mayonnaise, unless in large amounts, will not alter the consistency radically. However, a liquidizer mayonnaise, which is naturally thinner, may become nearer to a pouring sauce. This type of mayonnaise is ideal for folding into foods (such as vegetables) which will glisten with a fine shiny coating.

● Orange or lemon juice (in addition to lemon or vinegar used in the basic mayonnaise) are both used to give a refreshingly tangy flavour. Use 15 ml [1 tablespoon] or more according to taste. The flavour of the fruit is barely perceptible, but the mayonnaise loses some of its richness. The grated zest of the fruit can also be used, which will make the flavour more pronounced. This is good with mixed vegetables, fruit and nut salads or cold white fish.

● Whipped cream folded into a mayonnaise is a creamy accompaniment to cold mixed vegetable selections or cold egg dishes. Use 45 ml [3 tablespoons] to 250 ml [½ pint].

Cold chicken pieces in a curry mayonnaise.

85

Substantial additions

●One small peeled and grated dessert apple and a little freshly grated horseradish folded into the mayonnaise is delicious with cold beef or smoked mackerel.

●Half a cucumber, seeded, peeled and grated plus 4-5 small tomatoes skinned, seeded and chopped plus a pinch of paprika with mayonnaise should be served with cold pork or bacon.

●To make an anchovy sauce to serve with cold white fish, pound 4-5 drained anchovy fillets, chop 2 hard-boiled eggs and fold into mayonnaise.

MANY WAYS WITH MAYONNAISE

Mayonnaise is one of the most adaptable sauces—it goes with fish, meat, rice, pasta and, in particular, with hot or cold vegetables. Here are just some suggestions for using mayonnaise.

●For a Russian salad, mix together 1 small raw cauliflower broken into florets, 45-60 ml [3-4 tablespoons] each of cooked diced potatoes, cooked beetroot and cooked peas. Add 4 chopped, stuffed olives and 3 chopped anchovy fillets and fold into equal quantities of basic mayonnaise and sour cream. Alternatively, put in the vegetables and the dressing in layers, with cooked beetroot at the bottom of the dish to prevent staining the rest of the ingredients.

●For a tuna salad, flake 175 g [6 oz] canned tuna fish. Dice 450 g [1 lb] unpeeled red-skinned apples and 4 celery sticks. Combine with a Chantilly sauce.

Ensaladilla is an hors d'oeuvre of summertime vegetables.

●For a broad bean hors d'oeuvre, serve hot broad beans with aioli.

●For a sandwich filling, mix grated cheese with mayonnaise and pile into crusty French bread (buttered if liked).

●When poaching fish such as turbot or brill, take out cooked fish and reduce the stock by boiling. Remove from the heat and stir in twice as much aioli as fish stock (fumet). Reheat carefully without boiling until it is piping hot. Pour the sauce over the fish and serve.

●Cut open baked potatoes and fill with a combination of sour cream, mayonnaise and chopped chives.

●For a Waldorf salad, finely dice 450 g [1 lb] apples, reserving one which should be sliced and sprinkled with lemon juice. Chop 5 celery sticks and 75 g [2 oz] shelled walnuts and fold into 150 ml [¼ pt] basic mayonnaise with the diced apples. Line a salad bowl with a washed and dried lettuce, pile the salad into the centre and surround with apple slices.

●For a continental salad, combine 225 g [½ lb] cold, cooked pasta shells with 75 g [3 oz] sliced frankfurter. Dress with 75 ml [3 fl oz] mayonnaise into which you have stirred 10 ml [2 teaspoons] curry paste.

●For winter special, chop 4 celery sticks, 50 g [2 oz] walnuts, 3 apples and fold in 45 ml [3 tablespoons] orange mayonnaise.

●For a summer dip, serve a dish of aioli with crudités—a selection of strips of carrot and celery, cauliflower florets, whole spring onions and strips of green pepper.

●Serve a rémoulade sauce with grilled sprats.

●For a sauce Riviera, mix 250 ml [½ pt] mayonnaise verte with 15 ml [1 tablespoon] each of finely chopped capers and anchovy fillets plus 50 g [2 oz] cream cheese. This makes an excellent sandwich spread or sauce for cold beef or chicken.

●For a delicious summer lunch dish make a mayonnaise aux fines herbes (with 15 ml [1 tablespoon] of two or more finely chopped fresh herbs). Then fold in cold, cooked and drained boil-in-the-bag smoked haddock. Surround the dish with sliced tomatoes, cucumber and hard-boiled eggs.

●A quick potato mayonnaise can be made by combining cold, cooked diced potatoes and home-made mayonnaise. For first-class results, dice steamed, peeled potatoes while still warm and mix with vinaigrette then, when potatoes are cold, cover them with mayonnaise to which you have added chopped chives. Chopped spring onions or chopped hard-boiled eggs and finely chopped anchovy fillets make superb additions.

●Serve orange-flavoured mayonnaise with cold grilled chicken and an undressed salad of orange and watercress.

ENSALADILLA

This 'little salad' is a delicious Spanish hors d'oeuvre of fresh summer vegetables, steamed until just

tender and served with a pungent aioli sauce. The method of making aioli differs from the basic mayonnaise in that the garlic is crushed and worked in with the egg yolk. The vegetables are prepared first to allow them to become cold. Steam the vegetables for best flavour, after first washing them carefully and paring and removing any damaged parts.

This salad may be served plain or on a lettuce leaf or, for a party, it may be placed in a shallow bowl and un-moulded so that it retains the bowl shape. Decorate with strips of pimento.

SERVES 4
100 g [$\frac{1}{4}$ lb] new potatoes
100 g [$\frac{1}{4}$ lb] young carrots
100 g [$\frac{1}{4}$ lb] broad beans
100 g [$\frac{1}{4}$ lb] French beans
100 g [$\frac{1}{4}$ lb] peas

For the mayonnaise:
1 large-sized egg yolk
1-2 garlic cloves
salt
150 ml [$\frac{1}{4}$ pt] oil

1 Prepare the vegetables. Scrub the potatoes and young carrots, top and tail French beans and pod the peas and broad beans. Chop potatoes and carrots into quarters.

2 Place the potatoes in a steamer and steam for 10 minutes.

3 Add the broad beans, carrots and peas. Steam for a further 5 minutes.

4 Add the French beans and steam for 10 minutes until all the vegetables are tender.

5 Remove the vegetables from the steamer and allow to cool.

6 Bring the mayonnaise ingredients to room temperature, by removing from the refrigerator for about one hour before use. Warm the bowl by immersing in hot water.

7 Peel and chop the garlic and crush with a little salt.

8 Beat the egg yolk in the bowl for 1-2 minutes before adding the garlic. Beat again.

9 Beat in about half the oil, very carefully, drop by drop, until the mayonnaise takes on a thick, creamy consistency.

10 Rest the bottle on the edge of the bowl and trickle in the rest of the oil, beating all the time.

11 Dice all the vegetables until they are the same size as the broad beans.

13 Pour the aioli over the vegetables and stir gently so that all are coated.

BEETROOT MAYONNAISE

 This mayonnaise is based on the classic Gribiche sauce, which is made with cooked egg yolks. The 1.5 ml [$\frac{1}{4}$ teaspoon] of mustard which usually goes into a mayonnaise is omitted here. Beetroot mayonnaise is particularly good with cold beef.

SERVES 4
450 g [1 lb] beetroot

For the mayonnaise:
3 eggs
salt
15 ml [1 tablespoon] French mustard
7-15 ml [$\frac{1}{2}$-1 tablespoon] lemon juice or vinegar
150 ml [$\frac{1}{4}$ pt] oil
30 ml [2 tablespoons] whipped cream

1 Cut off the green tops of the beetroot taking care not to cut the flesh. Discard.

2 Place in a saucepan, pour over enough cold water to cover and bring to the boil. Cover and simmer for 2 hours for small beetroot, 3-4 hours for larger ones.

3 Meanwhile, for the mayonnaise warm the bowl to room temperature, by leaving it out for one hour or immersing in hot water.

4 Hard boil the eggs, drain and peel them. Halve the eggs, take out the yolks and push through a nylon sieve into the bowl. Chop the whites of two of the eggs and reserve.

5 Add salt, mustard and vinegar or lemon juice to the egg yolks and beat them well for half a minute.

6 Beat in about half the oil, very carefully, drop by drop, until it becomes a thick, creamy consistency.

7 Rest the bottle on the edge of the bowl and trickle in the rest of the oil, beating all the time.

8 Drain the beetroot. When cool enough, peel and slice or dice.

9 When the mayonnaise is finished, fold in the chopped egg whites and cream and spoon over the beetroot.

Serve sliced beetroot with Gribiche mayonnaise as an accompaniment to cold beef.

SEAFOOD COCKTAIL

This classic favourite makes an attractive and easy-to-prepare first course for any meal. The piquant tomato-flavoured sauce is traditional for prawns but should not overpower them, so be frugal with the use of Tabasco. Save the outer leaves of the lettuce for use in another dish.

SERVES 4
1 lettuce
350 g [¾ lb] prawns or shrimps
paprika pepper
4 lemon wedges

For the mayonnaise:
1 large-sized egg yolk
salt
1.5 ml [¼ teaspoon] French or
   English mustard
7-15 ml [½-1 tablespoon] lemon
   juice or vinegar
150 ml [¼ pt] oil
few drops of Worcestershire
   sauce

dash of Tabasco sauce
30 ml [2 tablespoons] tomato
   ketchup
lemon juice

1 Wash and dry the lettuce leaves, then wrap in a clean towel. Finely shred the lettuce heart and crisp in the refrigerator.

2 Bring the mayonnaise ingredients to room temperature by removing them from the refrigerator for at least one hour before use. Warm the bowl by immersing in hot water.

3 Beat egg yolks in the bowl for 1-2 minutes before adding mustard and salt and vinegar or lemon juice. Beat again.

4 Beat in about half the oil, very carefully, drop by drop, until it becomes a thick, creamy consistency.

5 Rest the bottle on the edge of the bowl and trickle in the rest of the oil, beating all the time.

6 When the mayonnaise is finished, fold in the Worcestershire sauce, Tabasco and tomato ketchup. Season to taste with extra lemon juice and salt and white pepper.

7 Peel most of the prawns, reserving one or two unpeeled to garnish each serving. Fold the peeled prawns into the sauce.

8 Remove the lettuce from the refrigerator and line four round wine glasses with the shreds. Divide seafood mixture between them.

9 Finish with a pinch of paprika on top of each glass. Garnish with one or two prawns, set on the edge of each glass, and a wedge of lemon.

Variations

● For the prawns substitute the same weight of cooked crabmeat. Decorate the edge of the glasses with a thin slice of lemon.

● Use the prawn, shrimp or crabmeat mixture to stuff large tomatoes. Cut the top from each tomato and scoop out the seeds and most of the flesh, taking care not to pierce the walls of the shell. Fill with the seafood mixture and serve on a plate surrounded with lettuce and lemon wedges.

● Here's a more substantial dish. Replace mayonnaise seasonings with 5 ml [1 teaspoon] tomato purée. Hard boil 4 eggs, and halve them lengthways. Cook 125 g [¼ lb] rice and when cold toss in 45 ml [3 tablespoons] vinegar. Place the eggs cut side down on the rice. Spoon over prawns in mayonnaise sauce and garnish the edge of the dish with cucumber slices.

● For a mussel mayonnaise, omit the prawns and flavourings in the sauce. Grate 1 celeriac or chop 2 small celery sticks, 2 small red-skinned eating apples and 1 small gherkin. Thinly slice 1 apple and dip slices in lemon juice. Add the vegetables to the mayonnaise. Fold in 24 cooked mussels (if canned, make sure they are well drained) with 2.5 ml [½ teaspoon] ready-made mustard, a squeeze of lemon juice and 30-45 ml [2-3 tablespoons] whipped cream.

Sauces

egg and butter sauces

Hollandaise, béarnaise and their variations are the finest and most delicious sauces of classic French cookery. Luxuriously rich, they are the perfect accompaniment for grilled meats, poached fish, delicately steamed vegetables or soft-boiled eggs. Unfortunately, these sauces gained a reputation for being difficult to make and even the most experienced cooks have been known to quail before tackling them. However, once you understand the basic principles, fine butter sauces present no problems. Follow the step-by-step guide and you can't go wrong.

In French cookery, one of the first rules of sauce-making is to try to make the sauce from part of the main dish—the juice from the meat perhaps, or the water from the vegetables. Where no such base is present, as in the case of grilled meats, poached or steamed fish, steamed vegetables, rice, pasta and soft-boiled eggs, the resourceful French turn to fine butter sauces to add flavour and interest to the meal.

Fine butter sauces are a glorious emulsion of lemon juice, vinegar or wine, egg yolks and unsalted butter. The most famous of these sauces are hollandaise and béarnaise, classic names from the culinary lore of France.

Subtle and smooth, fine butter sauces enhance rather than drown the food they are served with. They are the classic accompaniment for salmon, plainly grilled steaks and lamb cutlets, steamed white fish, asparagus, artichokes, broccoli and other steamed or boiled green vegetables. Even humble soft-boiled eggs can be turned into a gourmet treat with a hollandaise or béarnaise accompaniment.

When making fine butter sauces, the aim is to produce a lukewarm, creamy smooth emulsion which barely holds its shape and is just thick enough to coat the back of the spoon. This might seem a complicated and hazardous business, but approach the sauce calmly, do everything carefully and little can go wrong.

The basic principle of making a fine butter sauce is to persuade egg yolks to hold fat in suspension. To help them do this and give the sauce flavour, a sharp base of lemon juice, wine or vinegar is used. The egg yolks are added to this, then the butter is beaten in, slowly and gently until a fine emulsion is formed. Add too much butter and the sauce will curdle. Let the sauce get too hot and the eggs will scramble. So, as you will see, the watchword is caution. Go carefully, follow the step-by-step guide and you will be delighted with the results of your efforts.

INGREDIENTS
Such delicately flavoured sauces deserve the finest ingredients.

The base
Purists say that hollandaise sauce should be made only from eggs, butter and lemon juice. The problem with this is that the end results are rather insipid, so modern versions of hollandaise use a reduction (boiled-down mixture) of dry white wine or white wine vinegar to give the sauce extra flavour. Allow 45 ml [3 tablespoons] dry white wine or white wine vinegar before reducing, for every 2 egg yolks.

Sauce béarnaise classically has a base of dry white wine, tarragon vinegar, shallots and a few leaves of fresh tarragon. Allow 45 ml [3 tablespoons] dry white wine, 30 ml [2 tablespoons] tarragon vinegar, 2 peeled and finely chopped shallots and four to five leaves of fresh tarragon for each 2 egg yolks. In the variations of hollandaise and béarnaise, the acid flavouring elements differ but the proportions remain the same.

The eggs
Large, fresh eggs should be used at room temperature. If you can get free-range eggs with deep yellow yolks, so much the better. The eggs must be separated, but don't waste the whites. Use them to make meringues, soufflé omelettes or whisk them until stiff and fold into scrambled egg to make it extra light.

The butter
Unsalted butter is best as the flavour is not so intrusive as that of the salted kind. Traditionally, 75 g [3 oz] butter is allowed per large egg yolk. These proportions are successful if you are an experienced and confident fine butter-sauce maker but for the beginner, it is much better to allow 50 g [2 oz] per egg yolk. This is the amount of butter the yolk will readily absorb; so it is wisest to use no more than this on your first attempt and so minimize the things that can go wrong and spoil the sauce.

Classic cookery books soften the butter, cut it into dice and add it, bit by bit, to the mixture of beaten egg yolks and acid reduction. Our method uses part cold butter and part melted butter which is added like oil to mayonnaise. The end result is exactly the same as if you follow the classic method, but you are much less likely to meet with disaster on the way.

Seasoning
When the sauce is thickened, it is seasoned with salt and pepper and lemon juice. Black pepper, although finest in flavour, is to be avoided, as it adds unpleasant black specks to the sauce. Fill your pepper grinder with white peppercorns instead. Do not however use the dust sold as white pepper. It will float rather nastily on the surface of your sauce. Lemon juice is stirred into the sauce just before serving—10 ml [2 teaspoons] gives the right amount of piquancy to the basic two-yolk sauce.

In hollandaise and béarnaise variations, freshly chopped herbs are sometimes added at this point.

EQUIPMENT
A double boiler or a basin whose rim will just fit over the top of the pan—so the base does not touch the water—is essential when making fine butter sauces. They are much too delicate to set directly over the heat.

To beat the sauce you need a balloon or sauce whisk. An electric mixer is not really suitable because fine butter sauces are not made in vast quantities and electric mixers do not cope well with small amounts. You also need a small pan for melting the butter and a second small pan for reducing the acid base of the sauce.

THE BASIC TECHNIQUE
The basic technique of making fine butter sauces can be divided into easy-to-follow stages. The amounts referred to here are the same as in the step-by-step recipe.

Fine butter sauces can be served with a wide variety of plainly cooked vegetables to add flavour and interest.

Making the reduction
When white wine or white wine vinegar is used for making hollandaise sauce, it must be reduced by rapid boiling so that the flavour is concentrated. The wine, vinegar, herb and shallot base for béarnaise is also reduced.

To make the reduction, put the ingredients in a small pan, chopping shallots and herbs, where used, as finely as possible. Set the pan over a fierce heat and allow to boil rapidly, until the liquid is reduced to about 30 ml [2 tablespoons]. Set this liquid aside to cool a little, straining it first if herbs and shallots have been added.

Preparing the double boiler
Prepare the double boiler by putting water in the lower half, making sure that the upper half does not reach the water level.

Alternatively, improvise with a basin that will fit snugly over the top of the rim of a pan. Never stand the basin on a trivet. Not only is this a rather unsteady arrangement when you are whisking, but you would only be able to get a very little water in the pan without it touching the basin.

When you have prepared the double boiler, place it over a low heat. At the same time, fill the sink with cold water. This may come in useful later should the sauce begin to curdle and require rapid cooling.

Preparing the butter
Cut off 25 g [1 oz] from the measured

butter and set it aside. Place the remaining butter in a saucepan with a lip and melt it gently over low heat. Pour it into a small jug and set aside in a warm but not hot place.

Preparing the eggs

Separate the eggs into a clean bowl, reserving the whites for use in other dishes. Remove the top part of the double boiler from the heat and put the egg yolks into the top part.

Adding the eggs

Whisk the eggs until they have thickened slightly. This will take about three minutes. Still away from the heat, add the cooled wine or vinegar reduction and beat for another half minute. Never, ever, add the reduction to the eggs while it is still hot. You will get a nasty scrambled effect.

Adding the butter

Divide the reserved cold butter in half. Cut both halves into dice and add half to the egg mixture. Place the top of the double boiler back over the bottom. The water underneath should be simmering gently. Beat slowly with a whisk for one to two minutes, making sure you scrape the mixture from the sides and bottom of the pan all the time. This is the most crucial part of the operation. It is essential that the water is not too hot. If it is, the mixture will thicken too fast

and become lumpy.

The mixture becomes smooth and forms a light cream on the wires of the whisk. When you begin to see the bottom of the pan between strokes, it is time to remove the pan from the heat.

Add the remaining half of the cold reserved diced butter. This will cool the yolks and stop them from over cooking. Whisk for about one minute, until the butter has been amalgamated with the sauce. Still away from the heat, start adding the melted butter, drop by drop at first, whisking all the time. Take care to incorporate the mixture from the sides and bottom of the pan or basin all the time.

The butter is added at this stage in the same way as oil in the early stages of making mayonnaise (see how in previous chapter). Never add more butter until the previous drop has been smoothly incorporated into the sauce and has slightly thickened it. If the butter is added too quickly, the egg yolks will reject it and that means the sauce will refuse to thicken.

When half the butter has been absorbed and the sauce is the consistency of thick cream, pour in the remaining butter in a slow, steady dribble, whisking all the time.

Seasoning

When all the butter has been added and the sauce is thick, season with

salt and white pepper. For extra flavour, you may also wish to add a squeeze of lemon juice at this stage.

COPING WITH EMERGENCIES

Should your sauce go wrong, there is no need to pour it down the drain. Quick action can usually save the day. Here is what to do.

Fast thickening

Should the sauce thicken too fast and begin to go lumpy before all the butter has been incorporated, plunge the base of the top part of the double boiler into cold water—a sink or bowl full, which you will have providently prepared in advance. Leave in the water for one minute, to allow the sauce to cool, then whisk hard to cool the yolks. When they are barely warm (test with a fingertip), return the double boiler to the heat, checking that the temperature of the water in the bottom part has fallen. Reduce the heat under the saucepan before continuing.

Sauce begins to curdle

If the mixture begins to show just a hint of curdling (dividing into blobs) it can be rescued by removing from the heat and beating in 5-10 ml [1-2 teaspoons] very cold water. Take the bottom pan off the heat to reduce the water temperature. Then slightly reduce the heat of the cooker before returning the pan to continue.

SERVES 4
45 ml [3 tablespoons] dry white
wine or white wine vinegar
100 g [¼ lb] unsalted butter

2 large eggs
salt
freshly ground white pepper
10 ml [2 teaspoons] lemon juice

1 Place white wine or white wine vinegar in small pan over fierce heat. Boil rapidly until reduced to 30 ml [2 tablespoons]. Cool.

5 Place the remaining butter in a heavy-based saucepan over low heat. Allow to melt then pour it into a small jug. Set aside.

6 Separate yolks from whites. Place yolks in a clean bowl. Reserve the egg whites in the refrigerator for other dishes.

7 Remove the top of the double boiler from the heat and place the egg yolks in the top. Whisk with a balloon or sauce whisk.

11 When the mixture becomes smooth and forms a light cream on the whisk, and you can see the pan base, remove from heat.

12 Add the remaining half of the solid butter and whisk for about 1 minute until the butter has amalgamated with the sauce.

13 Still off the heat, start adding the melted butter, drop by drop at first. Whisk all the time and scrape from sides and bottom.

hollandaise sauce

2 To prepare a double boiler put water in the lower half. Water must not touch upper half of the boiler. Set over low heat.

3 Put some cold water in the sink, or large-sized bowl, in case you need to cool the sauce rapidly later on.

4 Cut off 25 g [1 oz] of the butter. Divide this in half and cut into small dice. Keep the dice separate and leave in a cool place.

8 When the egg yolks are creamy, stop whisking and, still away from the heat, add the wine or vinegar. Whisk for another half minute.

9 Add half of the diced butter to the eggs. Return the top to the boiler over heat, checking that the water is just simmering.

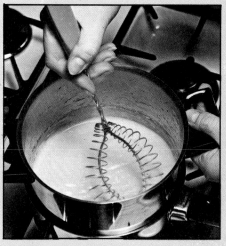

10 Begin whisking the sauce. Whisk slowly for 1-2 minutes, making sure you scrape the mixture from the sides and bottom of the pan.

14 When half the butter has been absorbed and the sauce is like thick cream, pour in the rest in a steady dribble, whisking well.

15 When all the butter has been added and the sauce is thick, season with salt and pepper. Stir in the lemon juice.

16 Transfer the sauce to a warmed (but not hot) sauce-boat and serve immediately. Hollandaise sauce is always served lukewarm.

Sauce separates

If the sauce separates into egg yolk and melted butter, remove it from the heat, empty into a bowl and wash out the top of the double boiler. Place a fresh egg yolk in the top of the double boiler, beat it then add the separated mixture a little at a time, beating well and keeping the heat low.

Sauce refuses to thicken

This is the result of adding butter too quickly. Rinse out a clean bowl with hot water, put 5 ml [1 teaspoon] lemon juice and 15 ml [1 tablespoon] of the thin sauce into this bowl. Whisk until it is creamy, then add the rest of the thin sauce a little at a time.

Sauce becomes too thick

If the sauce becomes too thick (remember, it should just hold its shape), remove it from the heat and beat in 15-30 ml [1-2 tablespoons] hot water, milk or cream.

Sauce turns to scrambled egg

This is the one occasion when nothing can be done to save the situation. Pour the mess down the drain and start again, working on a lower heat and with more caution this time.

PREPARING IN ADVANCE

Ideally, fine butter sauces should be prepared just before serving, but should you find yourself obliged to keep the sauce, for time reasons perhaps, it can be made an hour in advance. If you know you will have to keep the sauce warm, play safe by beating 5 ml [1 teaspoon] cornflour into the egg yolks at the beginning. This will stabilize the sauce.

When it is intended that the sauce should wait, stand the prepared sauce in a bain-marie (dish of warm water) allowing the water to come half way up the sides of the sauce container. Melt 25 g [1 oz] butter and whisk this in just before serving. Add seasoning and lemon juice.

Longer term storage

Hollandaise sauce may be stored in a screw-top jar in the refrigerator where it will keep for four days. This is a good idea if you want to serve cold meat later in the week. Make the sauce as described for advance preparation but do not add lemon juice and extra butter at the end. Allow the sauce to cool before placing it in a screw-top jar. It will set to a fairly solid butter in the refrigerator and will need to be reheated before serving.

To reheat the sauce, stand a basin in a bain-marie containing warm water. Add the sauce 30 ml [2 tablespoons] at a time and beat well until melted. When all the sauce has been melted, add 25 g [1 oz] butter as described in advance preparation and add lemon juice in the usual way.

USING A LIQUIDIZER

Fine butter sauces can be made in a liquidizer but instead of the usual quantities, 100 g [$\frac{1}{4}$ lb] butter is allowed for three egg yolks. Three egg yolks must be used as two is not sufficient to make a liquidizer sauce with this amount of butter. This means they do not have such a delicate flavour as sauces made in the classic manner. Fine butter sauce made using the usual ratio of butter to egg yolks would become so thick that the sauce would overheat the liquidizer motor.

One-speed liquidizers can be used to make fine butter sauces. If your liquidizer has several speeds, check with the instruction book. The speed for hollandaise and other fine butter sauces will be the same as for mayonnaise. For full details of making fine butter sauces in a liquidizer, see the step-by-step guide.

HOLLANDAISE VARIATIONS

There are several simple variations on the basic sauce hollandaise shown in the step-by-step guide. Their uses are given in the chart.
● For sauce mousseline, fold 50 ml [2 fl oz] whipped cream into the finished sauce.
● For sauce avec blanc d'oeufs, fold two stiffly beaten egg whites into the finished hollandaise.
● For sauce maltaise, use the juice and finely grated rind of a blood orange instead of the wine or vinegar base.
● For sauce divine, stir 15 ml [1 tablespoon] liquid made by reducing 30 ml [2 tablespoons] sherry, and 30 ml [2 tablespoons] whipped cream into hollandaise sauce.
● For sauce vin blanc, add 10 ml [2 teaspoons] reduced fish stock to the hollandaise sauce.

Step-by-step to hollandaise sauce in a liquidizer

1 First warm the goblet of your liquidizer. To do this, fill it with hot water, leave for 5 minutes, then rinse out and dry.

3 Place the butter in a heavy-based pan with a lip over low heat. Allow it to melt then pour into a small jug. Set aside.

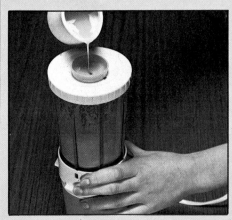

5 While blending, add the melted butter in a very slow trickle. When the sauce is thick, stop adding butter if not all used.

SERVES 4
45 ml [3 tablespoons] dry white
  wine or white wine vinegar
100 g [¼ lb] unsalted butter
3 large eggs
salt
freshly ground white pepper
10 ml [2 teaspoons] lemon juice

2 Meanwhile, place white wine or
wine vinegar in a small pan over
fierce heat. Boil until reduced to 30
ml [2 tablespoons]. Cool.

4 Separate the eggs and place the
yolks in the liquidizer goblet. Add
the reduction and blend for about 4
seconds until well mixed.

6 Season with salt, freshly ground
white pepper and lemon juice.
Blend for a further 10 seconds then
turn into a warmed sauce-boat.

SERVING FINE BUTTER SAUCES	
Sauce	**Serving suggestions**
HOLLANDAISE	Poached or grilled salmon steaks, asparagus, artichoke hearts, broccoli or calabrese.
Mousseline	With any of the above and with lamb cutlets.
Maltaise	With fried scampi, sole or plaice fillets. Also good with asparagus and broccoli.
Avec blanc d'oeufs	With poached and steamed white fish, broccoli and asparagus.
Divine	With chicken, sole, plaice.
BEARNAISE	With grilled steak, especially tournedos, shellfish and chicken.
Choron	With grilled fillet steaks, poached eggs and fish.
Foyot	Poached or soft-boiled eggs, veal sweetbreads.
Nivernaise	With grilled lamb cutlets, poached eggs, steaks, grilled chicken breasts.
Paloise	With grilled lamb cutlets.

SAUCE BEARNAISE

Sauce béarnaise is the sister of sauce hollandaise. It is very similar but thicker and stronger in flavour. It is used with grilled steaks and lamb chops, chicken and shellfish.

SERVES 4
45 ml [3 tablespoons] dry white
  wine
30 ml [2 tablespoons] tarragon
  vinegar
2 shallots
4-5 leaves of fresh tarragon
100 g [¼ lb] unsalted butter
2 large eggs
salt
freshly ground white pepper
10 ml [2 teaspoons] lemon juice
4-5 leaves freshly chopped
  tarragon (optional garnish)

1 Place the wine and vinegar in a
small pan.

2 Peel the shallots, chop finely and
add to the pan. Chop the tarragon
leaves and add to the pan.

3 Boil over fierce heat until reduced

to 30 ml [2 tablespoons]. Strain,
discard bits and pieces, and set
liquid aside to cool.

4 Prepare the double boiler and set
over low heat.

5 Cut off 25 g [1 oz] of the butter.
Divide this in half and cut each half
into dice.

6 Place the remaining butter in a
heavy-based saucepan over low
heat and melt.

7 Pour the melted butter into a small
jug. Leave in a warm place.

8 Separate the egg yolks.

9 Remove the top of the double
boiler from the bottom. Place the
egg yolks in this.

10 Whisk the egg yolks until slightly
creamy.

11 Add the reduction of wine and
vinegar to the egg yolks and whisk
for a further ½ minute.

12 Place the top of the double boiler back over the heat checking that the water is just simmering. Add half the diced butter.

13 Whisk the sauce for 1-2 minutes, making sure you scrape the mixture from the sides and bottom of the pan.

14 When the mixture becomes smooth and thick, and you can see the base of the pan between strokes, remove from the heat.

15 Now whisk in the rest of the cold butter. This will take about 1 minute.

16 Start adding the melted butter, drop by drop, whisking after each addition.

17 When the sauce is like thick cream, add the rest of the butter in a slow, steady dribble whisking all the time.

18 When all the butter has been added, season with salt and freshly ground white pepper.

19 Stir in the lemon juice. Chop the fresh tarragon leaves, if using and stir in.

Variations
There are many variations on sauce béarnaise. For their uses, see the chart.

●For sauce choron, stir 35 ml [1½ fl oz] tomato purée into the sauce just before serving.

●For sauce foyot, stir 30 ml [2 tablespoons] meat glaze or jelly from beneath good dripping into the sauce just before serving.

●For sauce nivernaise, work 1 clove of crushed garlic and 5 ml [1 teaspoon] finely chopped fresh parsley into the cold butter before adding to the eggs.

●For sauce paloise, replace the tarragon in sauce béarnaise with mint.

USING FINE BUTTER SAUCES
Although fine butter sauces may seem like a lot of trouble to make, they can be used in many ways.

●Mix cold sauce nivernaise with shredded florentine fennel or grated celeriac and serve as part of a cold hors d'oeuvre.

●For tournedos béarnaise, arrange grilled tournedos on a dish with small boiled new potatoes. Serve béarnaise sauce separately.

●For tournedos Henry IV, arrange grilled tournedos on fried croûtons. Place a cooked artichoke heart filled with thick béarnaise sauce on each. Garnish with grilled mushrooms and boiled baby new potatoes.

Tournedos Henri IV are classically served with béarnaise sauce.

●Fill the centre of globe artichokes with hollandaise sauce. As the leaves are pulled off, they are dipped into the sauce to be eaten.

●For a delicious salad, mix cold cooked sweetcorn and asparagus tips with sauce avec blanc d'oeufs.

●Make an economical meal more interesting! Serve lamb scrumpets with nivernaise sauce.

●For tournedos Helder, arrange grilled tournedos on croûtons. Place on each of the tournedos a ring of béarnaise sauce and in the middle of this, a spoonful of tomato purée. Garnish with baby new potatoes and grilled tomatoes.

●For eggs à la Beauharnais, soft boil eggs, arrest cooking, shell and place each egg on a warm, cooked artichoke heart. Mask with sauce divine.

●For a delicious yet economic first course, serve a mixture of boiled vegetables (such as broccoli, new potatoes, new carrots, young leeks) with hollandaise or mousseline sauce.

●Serve sauce divine with plain oeufs en cocotte.

●Use fine butter sauces to disguise and enhance cold meat. Paloise and nivernaise go with lamb; divine with chicken and turkey; maltaise with cold duck and game; choron goes especially well with beef.

Index

alcohol, sauce ingredient 72
aioli 84
anchovy mayonaise 86
  sauce 45
apple, curried soup 28
  mayonnaise flavouring 86
arrowroot thickening 41
artichoke and tomato soup 29
Avgolemono 9

bacon and green pea soup 21
bain-marie 42, 66, 70
balloon whisk 42
béarnaise sauce 95
béchamel cream soups 36
  sauce 42
beef broth 16
beetroot mayonnaise 87
Bercy sauce 56, 58
  fish in 58
Bigarade sauce 73
blanching veal bones 3
blanquette de veau 62
bones, stock 2
bouquet garni 3, 67
bourguignonne sauce 73
broths 11, 12
brown roux 68
  sauce 65, 68
  stock 2, 6, 66
butter muslin 4
  sauces 89

calves head stock 2
caper sauce 45
cauliflower cheese 49
celery sauce 45
Chantilly sauce 84
chasseur sauce 73
cheese sauce 45
cherry soup 27
chicken, Chinese mushroom soup 10
  cream soups 32, 40
  stock 2, 7
  vol au vent 48
Chinese chicken soup 10
  hot and sour soup 10
chinois strainer 66
Chivry sauce 56, 59
chocolate cream 51
  pears 50
choron sauce 95, 96
cider sauce 73
cock-a-leekie 13
colander 4
cold soups 25
combination soups 25
corn oil, mayonnaise ingredient 80
cornflower thickening 41
cream and egg liaison 54
  brown sauce ingredient 72
  mayonnaise enricher 85
cream-soup 31
  chicken 40
  fish 39
  lettuce 37
  method 34
  spinach 37-8
  vichyssoise 40
crème Dubarry 26
croûtons 14-15
cucumber and turnip soup 26
curdled butter sauces 91
  mayonnaise 83
curry, apple soup 28
  mayonnaise 85
  velouté sauce 56, 59

degreasing brown sauce 70

demi-glace 66
  sauce 77
dépouiller brown sauce 70
divine sauce 94, 95
double boiler 66, 70
dumplings, herb 16

egg à la Beauharnais 96
  cream liaison 54
  hard-boiled mayonnaise 85
  Hungarian 59
  mayonnaise 80
  sauce 45
  yolk, sauces 79
enriching cream soup 32, 34
  purée soup 25
ensaladilla 86
equipment, cream soups 32
  mayonnaise 80
  purée soups 24
  sauces 42
  stock-making 3-4
  velouté sauce 54
espagnole sauce 66, 70

fennel, fish stock 3
  vichyssoise 30
fines herbes sauce 73
fish, Bercy sauce with 58
  cream soups 32, 39
  stock 2, 7
  vol-au-vent 58
fond brun 66
foyot sauce 95, 96
freezing cream soup 36
  roux 44
  velouté sauce 57
French onion soup 20
fruit, brown sauce ingredients 72
  mayonnaise ingredient 85, 86
  purée soups 26

game stock 2, 7
garlic mayonnaise 84
  velouté sauce 56, 58
garnishes, brown sauce 72
  cream soup 36
gazpacho 28
green pea & bacon soup 21
Gribiche sauce 84

half-glaze 66
ham and leeks au gratin 48
herbs, brown sauce ingredients 72
  dumplings 16
  mayonnaise flavourings 85
  stock 3
  velouté sauce 56
hollandaise sauce 92-3
  liquidizer method 94
  household stock 2, 7
Hungarian eggs 59

italienne sauce 74

Jerusalem artichoke soup 29
juniper, sauce ingredient 71
jus lié 65, 68

kedgeree 49

leeks, au gratin with ham 48
lemon balm 3
  juice in mayonnaise 80, 85
  verbena 3
lettuce cream soup 38
liaison, egg and cream 54
liquidizer, hollandaise sauce 95
  mayonnaise 83

sauces 42
  vegetable purée 24
loin chops with sauce Robert 76
lyonnaise sauce 74

Madère sauce 74
maltaise sauce 94, 95
marjoram in stock 3
mayonnaise 79
  curdled 83
  method 80-83
  verte 84
measuring jug 54
melon soup 30
minestrone 16
mistakes, butter sauces 91
  Hollandaise sauce 94
  mayonnaise 83
  sauces 46
Mornay sauce 45
moules à la marinière 18
mousseline mayonnaise 84
  sauce 94, 95
mussel broth 18
  mayonnaise 88
mushroom, Chinese chicken soup 10
  sauce 45
  velouté sauce 56, 59
mustard, brown sauce ingredient 72
  demi-glace sauce 74
  mayonnaise ingredient 80
  sauce 45

nivernaise sauce 95, 96

oil, mayonnaise ingredient 80
olive oil, mayonnaise 80
onion, poulette sauce with 60
  sauce 45
  soup, French 20
orange flavoured mayonnaise 86
oxtail broth 15

paloise sauce 95, 96
Panada sauce 44
paper, kitchen 4
paprika velouté sauce 56, 59
  egg with 61
parlsey sauce 45
pea soup 28
pears, chocolate sauce with 50
Périgueux sauce 71
pig's trotters stock 2
poivrade 71
Polonaise sauce 56, 58
pork chops with sauce Robert 76
potage Crecy 28
poulette sauce 56, 58
  onion with 60
  prawn sauce 45
purée fruit soups 26
  vegetable soups 22

redcurrant jelly, sauce ingredient 71
re-heating brown sauces 70
  velouté sauce 57
  white sauces 42
rémoulade 84
riviera sauce 86
Robert sauce 74
  chops with 76
rodgrod 51
Romaine sauce 74
rosemary in stock 3
Rouennaise sauce 74
roux-based sauces 42
  brown 68
Russian salad 86

salad cream 79
sauce à la diable 73
  avec blanc d'oeufs 94, 95
  espagnole 66, 70
  mère 41, 53
  Robert 74, 76
  whisk 42
sandwich filling 86
saucepans 42
Scotch broth 13
seafood cocktail 88
sieve, conical 54, 66
  nylon mesh 66
  sauces 42
  vegetable purée 24
skimmer 4
spatula 42
spices, brown sauce ingredients 72
spinach cream soup 37-8
spoon, perforated 4
  wooden 42
stock, brown 6, 66
  chicken 7
  fish 7
  household 7
  method 4
  pan 4
  storing 46
  types 2
  uses 2
  vegetable 8
  white 6
storing brown sauces 70
  cream soup 36
  hollandaise sauce 94
  mayonnaise 83
  purée soups 25
  roux 44
  stock 4, 6
  velouté sauce 57
stracciatella 10
suprême sauce 56, 58
sweating vegetables 23
sweet sauces 46

tarragon sauce 45
  stock 3
tartare sauce 84
thin soups 9
tournedos Helder 96
truffles, sauce ingredient 71
tuna salad 86
turnip and cucumber soup 26

veal, blanching 3
  blanquette 62
  bone stock 2
vegetable, brown sauce
  ingredients 67, 72
  cream soups 32
  mill 24
  purée soups 22
  stock 2, 3, 8
velouté sauce 53-5
  recipes 58
venaison sauce 71
vichyssoise 40
  fennel 30
vin blanc sauces 94, 95
vinegar, brown sauce ingredient 72
  mayonnaise ingredient 80
vol-au-vents, chicken 48

Waldorf salad 86
walnut soup 30
whisk 42, 54
white roux-based sauces 42-5
  stock 2, 4, 6
wooden spoon 42